Community collaboration and differential response:
Canadian and international research and emerging models of practice

Nico Trocmé, Della Knoke, and Catherine Roy, Editors

Centre of Excellence for Child Welfare | Centre d'excellence pour la protection et le bien-être des enfants

National Library of Canada Cataloguing in Publication

National Child Welfare Symposium on Community Collaboration and Differential Response (4th : 2003 : Banff, Alta.)
    Community collaboration and differential response: Canadian and international research and emerging models of practice/Nico Trocmé, Della Knoke, and Catherine Roy, editors.

Includes proceedings from the 4th National Child Welfare
    Symposium on Community Collaboration and Differential
    Response, sponsored by the Centre of Excellence for Child
    Welfare and the Alberta Ministry of Children's Services, held
    Mar. 20–21, 2003, in Banff, Alta.
Includes bibliographical references.
ISBN 1-896297-13-7

    1. Community-based child welfare—Canada. 2. Community-based family services—Canada. 3. Community-based child welfare. 4. Community-based family services.
I. Trocmé, Nicolas Maurice, 1959- II. Knoke, Della, 1964- III. Roy, Catherine, 1973-
IV. Child Welfare League of Canada. V. Alberta. Alberta Children's Services VI. Centre of Excellence for Child Welfare. VII. Title.

HV713.N37 2003   362.7'0971   C2003-907044-1

© Child Welfare League of Canada, 2003

Également disponible en français sous le titre : *Collaboration communautaire et approches différentielles : recherches et pratiques novatrices canadiennes et internationales*

Design and layout by Leah Gryfe

The Centre of Excellence for Child Welfare is one of the Centres of Excellence for Children's Well-Being funded by Health Canada. The CECW is also funded by Canadian Institutes of Health Research and Bell Canada. The views expressed herein do not necessarily represent the official policy of Health Canada.

 Health Canada Santé Canada

The Centre gratefully acknowledges Alberta Children's Services and IBM Canada for co-sponsoring the 4th National Child Welfare Symposium: Community Collaboration and Differential Response, held in Banff, AB in March 2003. Alberta Children's Services and IBM Canada worked in partnership with the Centre of Excellence for Child Welfare to bring together researchers and practitioners from Canada, the United States, and the United Kingdom with the best available information about innovative approaches and alternative models of child welfare service delivery.

For information about the Centre of Excellence for Child Welfare, visit *www.cecw-cepb.ca*.
Copies of this publication are available at cost from:

    Centre of Excellence for Child Welfare
    c/o Child Welfare League of Canada
    209 – 75 Albert Street
    Ottawa, ON K1P 5E7
    Tel.: (613) 235-4412, ext 24
    Email: *info@cecw-cepb.ca*

Table of Contents

Foreword
Peter Dudding v

Introduction
Nico Trocmé, Della Knoke, and Catherine Roy vii

Part 1: Research and policy
New directions in child welfare
*Provincial and Territorial Directors of Child Welfare,
with editing by Jay Rodgers* 1

Avenues for positive innovations in Canadian child welfare:
Lessons from the Partnerships for Children and Families Project
and international jurisdictions
Gary Cameron, Nancy Freymond, and Catherine Roy.................. 14

Re-involving the community: The need for a differential response
to rising child welfare caseloads in Canada
Nico Trocmé and Claire Chamberland 32

Evaluating the implementation of assessment tools in the Australian
child protection system
Jim Barber and Della Knoke 49

Alternative response to child protective services investigations
in the United States
Diana English, John D. Fluke, and Ying-Ying T. Yuan 64

Mobilizing communities to prevent child abuse and neglect:
A cultural shift in child protection
Liesette Brunson and Camil Bouchard 75

Part 2: Emerging models
Community based child welfare services in Guelph
and Wellington County
Maurice D. Brubacher and Jasma Narayan 89

Alberta Response Model: Transforming outcomes
for children and youth
Suzanne Anselmo, Russ Pickford, and Phil Goodman 98

USMA: Cherished ones, precious ones, the children
A First Nations approach to child, family, and community well-being
Debra Foxcroft and Cindy Blackstock *105*

The inclusive approach of the Outaouais Centres jeunesse
Gilles Clavel, Luc Cadieux, and Catherine Roy *112*

Integrating children's services: A perspective from England
Helen Jones, Ellen Chant, and Harriet Ward *119*

References *132*

Contributors *145*

Foreword

Peter Dudding

Is child welfare truly an enigma wrapped inside a riddle? For many of its planners and practitioners, it must seem to be, as many strategies to reform child welfare encounter significant difficulties and have unplanned results.

Managing change in child welfare is complicated and complex. It is complicated in that there are many interdependent variables both inside and outside the system that affect the safety and well-being of children and families. It is complex in that we know a great deal about successful approaches to raising children and supporting families but our knowledge is limited and there are significant information gaps. Even with the best available knowledge there are both predicted and unintended consequences of reform. Managing a child welfare system is part art and part science, much like raising a child.

The current emphasis on child protection in Canadian child welfare has dominated policy and practice for the past decade. The shift in emphasis originated from public concerns about the safety of children living in high risk families and has spread quickly throughout Canada, United States, and England. Most jurisdictions have implemented improved standards of child protection, focused training for child welfare workers, and risk assessment tools. While family preservation approaches were being discredited, access to a range of community-based services for families in need were also being limited due to a lack of funding. The "better safe than sorry" approach to child welfare has significantly increased the number of children in public care in Canada. Further, the focus on child protection has had an isolating effect, shifting the emphasis to the family court and management of growth within organizations. Currently, there is increasing concern within Canada about fundamental questions of the sustainability of child protection services, due to the growing demands for funding, human resources, and substitute care. There are also questions about whether we are helping children or further victimizing them through child protection interventions and if we are improving the quality of life outcomes for children growing up in substitute care.

Child welfare policy and practice have largely been influenced by values and ideology, experience, and the resources available. To date, the influence of research and evidence-based practice has been limited, although a growing body of social science research in Canada and internationally is beginning to have some positive effect. It is of critical importance that child welfare policy makers and practitioners place greater emphasis on research, evaluation and outcome methodologies to gain a better understanding of the complicated and complex aspects of child welfare services.

At the Community Collaboration and Differential Response symposium in Banff, Alberta on March 20 and 21, 2003, information was presented regarding innovations in First Nations, Canadian, American and English child welfare practice. A common theme was the development of approaches predicated upon the idea that child protection is a community responsibility. This involves the development of an effective network of formal and informal community partners, distinguishing between high and low risk situations, and providing a wider range of services responsive to the different needs of children and families.

These initiatives have tremendous potential and promise for creating a "virtuous cycle" of child welfare services, promoting optimal child development, family strengths, and positive communities. However, integral to their design is thoughtful and well conceived applied research programs to provide a critical evaluation of effectiveness and outcomes.

Increasing our knowledge and understanding of what works in child welfare and of the broader trends and patterns will enhance our ability to manage a human services system that is both complicated and complex.

Introduction

Nico Trocmé, Della Knoke, and Catherine Roy

Child welfare services across Canada are responding to growing numbers of referrals involving an increasingly broad array of problems. The increase has been driven primarily by cases involving neglect or exposure to domestic violence, while severe physical harm and sexual abuse represent a declining proportion of cases. Although urgent protective responses continue to be a priority in situations involving severe abuse, the majority of children and families who come to the attention of child welfare are ineligible for services under the narrow child protection mandate that characterizes the current system. There is growing interest in developing responses that are more effective in meeting the diverse needs of maltreated children through effective collaboration with other community service providers.

Differential response models, sometimes referred to as alternative response models or multi-track systems, have been implemented in jurisdictions in the United States, Australia, and most recently, in Alberta, Canada. These models include a range of potential response options customized to meet the diverse needs of families reported to child welfare. Differential response systems typically use multiple "tracks" or "streams" of service delivery, with at least one investigative track for high-risk cases and an alternative "assessment" or "community" track for less urgent cases, where the focus of intervention is on brokering and coordinating other community services to address the short- and long-term needs of children and families.

Systematic evaluation of the impact of differential response models is at an early stage. While there have been some positive results, the value of differential response is contingent upon engaging accessible and effective community resources. In an effort to examine emerging models in Canada and internationally, the Centre of Excellence for Child Welfare (CECW) in collaboration with the Alberta Ministry of Children's Services, with additional funding from IBM and Health Canada, held a two-day research and policy forum in Banff, Alberta in March 2003. The CECW's *4th National Child Welfare Symposium on Community Collaboration and Differential Response*, presented in partnership with Alberta Children's Services and IBM Canada, brought together senior policy makers from across Canada with researchers and service providers from Canada, the United States,

England, and Australia. Information presented at the symposium has been compiled in this publication and appears in two sections.

The first section describes key policy and research issues that have emerged from efforts to develop community collaboration and differential response models in child welfare. The first three chapters discuss the limitations of the current system and document the need for change. The opening chapter, by the provincial and territorial Directors of Child Welfare with editing by Jay Rodgers, provides a historical and policy context for the development of child welfare alternative response models. Shifts in funding structures, growing caseloads, and an increasingly risk adverse environment are creating an impasse. Investigation and evidence gathering take precedence and the lion's share of resources, at the expense of direct services for children and families. The voices of parents and service providers echo these concerns in the chapter by Cameron, Freymond, and Roy and argue for a more positive, strengths-based approach to serving children and families in difficulty. Drawing upon lessons learned from a project implemented in Ontario and from successful international experiences, the authors highlight possible avenues for more positive child welfare outcomes. These include increased collaboration between formal and informal partners working with children and families and reforming mandated child protection agencies. Reviewing service trend data from across Canada, Trocmé and Chamberland argue that urgent protective responses are required only for a small portion of child welfare cases. Non-urgent cases, however, are equally in need of services to ensure the long-term well-being of children. Coordinated community-based services that can address long-term needs are required through more collaborative responses that do not alienate other professionals and community partners as a result of rapid and intrusive investigations.

Although the need to shift away from narrowly focused protection models is clear, there are several key challenges in developing alternative approaches. Differential response models require the reliable differentiation between urgent high-risk situations and less urgent situations. Barber and Knoke's analysis of decision-making tools used in Australia to classify child protection cases into different response tiers shows they do not automatically lead to reliable decisions. Pilot testing and post-implementation evaluation revealed that the assessment processes and instruments were not implemented entirely as intended. This chapter documents the processes used to assess the application of decision-making criteria and the validity of priority ratings.

The widespread application of alternative response models in the United States has led to a number of critical implementation issues described by English, Fluke, and Yuan. Evaluation of alternative response services (ARS) implemented in Washington State found that a minority of the ARS families actually engaged in services and that the rate of re-referral among families receiving ARS was comparable to families not served or families receiving child protection services "as usual." This chapter underscores the need for systematic evaluation to determine the extent to which differential response services are meeting their intended objectives. In their chapter on community mobilization, Brunson and Bouchard look beyond the child welfare system to neighbourhoods and broader community groups which are instrumental in bringing about the type of cultural and attitudinal changes required to ensure that children and parents become community priorities. Through a review of past and current initiatives, the authors highlight some key elements required to mobilize communities so that strong and sustainable structures can be put in place to ensure the protection and well-being of all children and their families. After discussing some inherent difficulties and dilemmas associated with community mobilization, this chapter concludes that by combining efforts and pluralistic expertise—both formal and informal—maximal child protection becomes an attainable goal.

The second section of the book presents five innovative Canadian and British initiatives developed to provide more flexible and collaborative approaches to child welfare practice. Brubacher and Narayan present a number of community programs developed by the Family and Children's Services of Guelph and Wellington County in Ontario. Through these initiatives, families in difficulty are identified earlier, provided with more prevention services, and community resources are mobilized to avoid unnecessary placements of children in out-of-home care. This chapter illustrates that children, families, communities, and service providers can benefit substantially from community based child welfare services. Anselmo, Pickford, and Goodman present the Alberta Response Model, a province-wide initiative that includes a new differential response option for child welfare services as well as enhanced investments and emphasis on accessing community-based programs. Foxcroft and Blackstock describe the development of the Nuu-chah-nulth First Nation's community-based child welfare program in British Columbia and highlight the challenges encountered when establishing Aboriginal child welfare services within the limits of provincially imposed legislation and a federally imposed funding framework. Clavel, Cadieux, and Roy present a series of community based collaborations developed in the Outaouais region of southwestern Quebec. Through a strong commitment to developing individualized service plans for each youth referred to the protection authorities and well-developed service protocols with community programs, the Outaouais program has achieved one of Quebec's highest rates of diversion to alternative services. Finally, Jones, Ward, and Chant argue that child welfare agencies alone cannot be responsible for meeting all the needs of vulnerable children and families. The authors present an integrated child assessment framework developed in North Lincolnshire, England, which ensures that all service providers approach families from a common perspective and that children and families have access to better coordinated services and supports.

Inherent in the renewed emphasis on community collaboration and differential response is the promise of alternatives to a Canadian child welfare system narrowly focused on protection investigations. From the chapters included in this book a consensus emerges about the value of partnerships among child protection agencies, medical services, education resources, community based organizations and communities themselves, to ensure not only the maximal protection of children but maximal opportunities for optimal development and self-enrichment. Effective service innovation is facilitated by knowledge of the strengths and limitations of the program options available and an understanding of the implementation process and the obstacles encountered. The innovative programs described here demonstrate that child welfare systems can develop more flexible service approaches and make better use of community resources. It is important, however, to keep in mind the implementation issues identified by English, Fluke, and Yuan in the United States and by Barber in Australia. Reliable methods must be implemented and tested to ensure that children and families are referred to the appropriate service track. Service protocols and adequate resources must be put in place to ensure that services are indeed provided. Intervention must be evaluated to ensure that the services provided lead to positive outcomes for children and families. As stated by Brunson and Bouchard, we must learn from the constraints and dilemmas associated with past experiences and build on their strengths to develop even more successful programs. Successful collaborations require time and energy.

The initiatives presented at the *4th National Child Welfare Symposium on Community Collaboration and Differential Response* show tremendous potential for improving child welfare services in Canada. The Centre of Excellence for Child Welfare is committed to supporting these initiatives through research and evaluation. Critical analysis and systematic evaluation of emerging models and services contribute to the development of a system that provides effective responses to the diverse needs of maltreated children. But to build such a system, investments of time, resources, and energy must converge. The following chapters suggest that the time is right for all institutions devoted to the protection and well-being of children—be they universities, funding agencies, governments, child welfare agencies, or community based organizations—to move towards that "new direction" in child welfare.

New directions in child welfare

Provincial and Territorial Directors of Child Welfare, with editing by Jay Rodgers

Abstract

This chapter presents an historical overview of the major paradigm shifts in delivering child welfare services in Canada, including the child rescue era, the family preservation era and more recently, a renewed focus on child protection. These shifts are examined within the context of the social, economic, and intergovernmental factors that influenced change. The paper argues that while child welfare legislation in Canada has evolved over time, certain environmental factors have prevented the delivery systems from keeping pace with the core intent of the legislative changes. Common to all eras is that governments struggle with how best to meet the range of needs of children and families referred to the child welfare system. Within the narrow "better safe than sorry" mandate that characterizes the current system, workload pressures have increased as have the number and complexity of family needs. Services tend to be organized to respond to allegations of physical and sexual abuse, although neglect and emotional maltreatment account for the majority of substantiated cases. A disproportionate amount of time is spent on investigation and the collection of evidence to mobilize protective services, while the vast majority of cases are closed at intake, with no services provided. The current "one size fits all approach," like those that preceded it, fails to recognize the diverse set of needs that characterize children and families referred to child welfare services. A "narrowing plus" strategy is advocated to provide a broader and more flexible set of responses.

Early child welfare legislation in Canada and the extension of state authority

Prior to Confederation, there was no legislation in Canada specifically intended to deal with the problem of abused or neglected children. Children were seen as smaller versions of adults and as the exclusive property of their parents without their own special needs or rights. The British

North America Act (BNA Act) of 1867 established the legal context for the child welfare law in Canada. Provinces were given exclusive legislative jurisdiction in the fields of health, education, and welfare including authority over child welfare. The BNA Act gave the federal government superior taxing power and exclusive responsibility for certain classes of subjects including "Indians and lands reserved for Indians" (Constitution Act, 1867). These constitutional provisions were to have significant implications for the future development of child welfare services in the provinces.

Child welfare law in Canada began to take shape after Confederation. The impact of the industrial revolution in Canada (1880 to 1900) radically changed the nature of work and forever altered the roles of family members. New social ills associated with living in an urban industrialized capitalist environment arose and society began to recognize that children were not just small adults. The earliest legislation placed restrictions on the use of child labour and had provisions for the use of industrial residential schools to house orphaned or abandoned children. By the late 1880s, provinces began to pass new legislation based on a child protection philosophy. These statutes established the concept of *parens patriae* giving power to the state to act as a substitute parent and intervene into the usual parent-child relationship. Children were no longer seen as the exclusive property of their parents. The laws recognized the collective responsibility of society to care for children. By the early part of the twentieth century, most provinces had passed child welfare legislation based on the *parens patriae* principle.

Post World War II expansion in social policy

Child welfare legislation continued to develop throughout the twentieth century with the courts providing interpretation and clarification of the state's authority. A critical part of this evolution was a continuing refinement of what constitutes acceptable and unacceptable behaviour on the part of parents.

The 1950s and 1960s ushered in a new and unprecedented expansion of the social safety net in Canada. This era was marked by ever-increasing use of the federal government's spending power in areas that, constitutionally, were considered within the jurisdiction of the provinces. For child welfare, the most significant development occurred in 1966 when the federal government made funding available under the Canada Assistance Plan (CAP).

CAP offered full 50/50 cost sharing (with no limits) to the provinces and territories in areas where federal dollars had never before been available. One of those areas was child welfare. CAP also allowed, for the first time, federal funding for a variety of other provincial programs intended to support children and their families (e.g., day care, counselling, crisis intervention, family therapy, residential care).

What made CAP so important from a social policy perspective was not so much the availability of federal funding, but the conditions attached to that funding. It was through the use of these conditions that the federal government was able to exert influence on the design of provincial programs. This influence is known as the "federal presence" in provincial jurisdiction programs. The impact of the federal presence on the continued evolution of child welfare should not be overlooked. The following are germane to child welfare.

- The availability of federal cost-sharing acted as an incentive for provinces to expand their social service infrastructure. Provinces directed resources into those programs that would qualify for CAP funding. For child welfare, the CAP conditions were biased toward a system that emphasized substitute care.
- Development did not occur as rapidly for those services that were ineligible for CAP recoveries, limiting the availability of important support services.
- The CAP exclusion of related programs (i.e., corrections, education, and health) discouraged the development of an integrated service environment. Child welfare emerged as a stand-alone service system somewhat in isolation from other important programs.
- While the availability of some family support services expanded under CAP, provinces tended to organize these other programs separately from child welfare with their own administration and governance structures.

While the availability of CAP funding resulted in a general expansion of social programming, as a specific component of this, child welfare evolved in isolation from other systems and with a concentration on legal child protection service delivered under direct control of the state. Within this context in the mid 1960s, "the battered child syndrome" (Kempe et al., 1962) emerged from the medical profession to capture the attention of governments and their child welfare administrators. The focus on physical abuse had an important impact on the specific manner in which child welfare systems expanded within the new CAP funding environment. The battered child syndrome represents child physical abuse as an escalating problem and defines the problem as a medical syndrome requiring a disease prevention model structured around early detection and reporting.

The trend now was for child welfare systems to focus on abuse allegations with the allocation of resources prioritized for the functions of investigation and verification. Child physical abuse became a major driver of child welfare activity. Society's growing awareness and intolerance of child abuse led to increased pressure on child welfare authorities to seek out, gather evidence, and then "rescue" children from abusive situations. Service delivery agents were now, more than ever, expected to act in accordance with the more interventionist and intrusive aspects of the *parens patriae* principle. Frequently, the rescue approach meant that the child was placed into substitute care away from the alleged perpetrators. The number of children in substitute care increased dramatically throughout the remainder of the 1960s and continued in the 1970s.

Paradigm shift in child welfare: The era of family preservation

By the early 1980s, the rescue approach was coming under heavy criticism and increased scrutiny. First Nations' leadership lobbied government to end the "sixties scoop" (a term for the removal of large numbers of Aboriginal children from their communities for placement in non-Aboriginal families) approach and give their communities the authority to care for their own children. Consumer rights movements also played a role across North America in questioning the "state knows best" approach to child welfare. The importance of children's rights was recognized internationally through the United Nations Convention on the Rights of the Child and, in Canada, by incorporating them into the Canadian Charter of Rights and Freedoms.

Child welfare systems were also under increased scrutiny from within the internal workings of government. Provincial governments were concerned with the ever-increasing budget demands arising from their child welfare systems. The wisdom of choosing the most intrusive and expensive service option (i.e., substitute care) was being questioned within government circles.

Provincial governments responded by altering the legislative environment. A new philosophy emerged as many provinces passed new acts that adopted a civil liberties emphasis rather than the paternalistic state authority approach. This ushered in the era of child and family services statutes. The new laws focused on children's rights and family preservation as the preferred response for fulfilling the child protection mandate. Emphasis was placed on the principles of family support, prevention, and the least intrusive intervention. Child welfare systems were now expected to address a whole new set of child-specific and family issues not previously within the scope of their legislative responsibilities (e.g., fetal alcohol syndrome, addictions, learning disabilities, mental health).

Initially, the results were encouraging as the number of children in care declined throughout the 1980s and First Nations agencies emerged to deliver statutory services within their reserve communities. This trend did not continue however, as child welfare delivery systems were not able to evolve in a manner consistent with the ideological shift in the legislation. With significant fiscal challenges at hand, provincial governments were unable to inject enough new resources to allow their child welfare authorities to meet the increased demand that came with the broadened mandate. Collateral service systems were not able to fill in the gaps as these programs had experienced years of underfunding. Without being able to provide sufficient supports to address safety concerns, workers often had no alternative but to bring the child into care.

Other external factors during the 1980s put increased pressure on the front end of the system. Child sexual abuse gained national attention and heightened public pressure for more state intervention to protect children. Increased recognition and understanding by child welfare workers of the dynamics of child sexual abuse created new challenges for the intake process. Combined with a number of high profile child deaths, this resulted in child welfare systems coming under an unprecedented public scrutiny. During this time period the full impact of the Charter was also being felt as the courts set new expectations for the burden of proof and due process in legal proceedings to terminate parental rights.

Within the context of these environmental factors, child abuse again emerged as a key influence of system design causing the service philosophy to shift back to a child protection mandate. By the end of the 1980s, the legislative pendulum had shifted toward family preservation but, rather than expanding services to support families, child welfare systems were pushed by environmental pressures to narrow their mandate and re-focus on child protection, investigation, and gathering evidence. The "better safe than sorry" philosophy prevailed.

Environmental context in the 1990s: The funding situation worsens

By the early to mid 1990s, it was evident that the initial successes of the family preservation era were short lived. The number of children in care was again beginning to rise steadily in most provinces. This put even more pressure on already strained child welfare budgets. The situation worsened in 1995 when the federal government replaced CAP with the Canada Health and Social Transfer (CHST). The CHST combined all federal cost-sharing for health, post-secondary education, social assistance, and social services into one "super block" transfer. The amount of the block was determined by a set formula and was drastically less than what the provinces would have received previously.

Incorporating CAP into a block fund had important implications for child welfare. Under the CAP model of full financial partnership, as demand for services rose and provinces spent more money, the federal government would cover 50% of all eligible costs. This was no longer the case under the CHST. This is particularly difficult for statutory programs like child welfare in which mandated providers are required by law to deliver certain services. Provinces are forced to pick up an ever greater proportion of the increased costs as the federal contribution remains stable and impervious to the service realities.

The CHST single fund forced provinces to prioritize the allocation of limited dollars between health, post-secondary education, and social services. Social services had to compete for resources with programs like health that have a very high level of political and public support. The CHST created a fixed funding environment in which social services were de-prioritized when making decisions about how finite funding would be distributed among programs. Many support services for families fell victim to funding cuts resulting from the withdrawal of federal cost-sharing.

Service delivery trends in the 1990s: What are the implications?

By the mid 1990s, child welfare systems around the country were struggling to exist within a volatile environment. There was a clear and worsening divide between the wide parameters and family support values of the legislation, and the funding constraints, external pressures, and child protection focus of service delivery. Within this environment, certain trends in child welfare emerged throughout the 1990s and continue to influence service delivery in the twenty-first century. The most significant trends and challenges are discussed below.

1. Service design challenges

Provinces have struggled somewhat to find the best organizational configuration for their delivery systems. Throughout the 1990s, provinces tended to focus on structure rather than on clarity of mandate. Models have varied around the country based on the degree of centralization and devolution of authority. In some provinces, the extension of First Nations' authority has further complicated system design.

2. Increasing number of referrals

A variety of factors (e.g., expanded legislative mandate, cuts in collateral services) have led to a tremendous increase in referrals. Child welfare has become a catch-all system that is expected to respond to all kinds of family issues. Recent studies suggest that child welfare has continued to focus on the child protection mandate. Nationally, approximately 70% of all referrals to child welfare agencies are closed at intake or after the initial assessment is completed and no services provided, regardless of whether those families would have benefited from receiving some type of support services.

3. Focus on investigation and evidence building

The delivery of child welfare services in the 1990s focused on the child protection aspect of the mandate. There is significant pressure to hold the system accountable and to ensure that due process is followed in any proceeding that may reduce parental rights. This has placed a particularly heavy burden on the front end of the system. Agencies have prioritized their limited resources to strengthen the intake and initial assessment process where the focus is on investigation and collecting evidence.

As part of the initial service response, there is an attempt to distinguish between referrals on the basis of priority. The expected outcome is a ranking of each referral based on the degree of risk to the child. This ranking then determines whether child welfare intervention should continue. In order to qualify for ongoing service, there must be evidence that a child has been or is at risk of being abused or neglected and that the parent is unable or unwilling to protect the child from that abuse or neglect. While the family's general need for service may also be considered, this is secondary to the main purpose of the investigation.

4. One size fits all response

The family preservation ideological shift, the least intrusive principle, periodic but intense public scrutiny, the impact of the Charter and higher proof standards being applied by the courts combined to increase the expectation that child welfare agencies clearly justify when intrusive action by the state is in the best interests of the child. In response, many jurisdictions have attempted to standardize the investigation and assessment processes to ensure that relevant and sufficient data are gathered in a consistent manner. This approach limits the flexibility of the service response. This tends to augment the investigation and protective oversight focus and makes it difficult for child welfare agencies to tailor their services to meet the unique needs of families. This "one size fits all" response assumes that families present with similar needs in similar circumstances.

5. Organized to respond to abuse allegations

Due mainly to society's intolerance of the physical and sexual abuse of children, many child welfare providers have built substantial service mechanisms designed to respond to allegations of abuse (e.g., specialized training programs, expert units, protocols, abuse committees, and multi-disciplinary service teams). Data from Canada's first national study on the incidence of child abuse and neglect may challenge the assumption that abuse is the key driver of referrals. The Canadian Incidence Study of Reported Child Abuse and Neglect (CIS) reveals that, in 1998, child neglect (40%) and emotional maltreatment (19%) were the primary drivers of referrals to child welfare agencies in Canada (59% of all referrals). Correspondingly, physical abuse (31%) and sexual abuse (10%) represented 41% of all referrals (Trocmé & Wolfe, 2001). Service response systems may be geared up for a response to an abuse allegation when neglect and emotional harm are actually the primary sources of referrals and the primary reason for case openings.

The CIS and other reports draw a connection between the incidence of neglect, income levels, and the stresses of being a single parent. Child welfare agencies are less equipped to address issues of poverty and lack of community based supports for single parents feeling isolated, than they are prepared to investigate and respond to allegations of abuse.

6. The state as substitute parent

Nationally, the number of children in the care of provincial and territorial child welfare authorities has grown since the early 1990s. While there are limited data in this area, there is a growing body of evidence to suggest that the state may not be a very good parent. Recent research indicates that children who "age out of the system" [or reach the age of independence, which ranges from 16 to 19 depending on the jurisdiction (Secretariat to the Federal/Provincial/Territorial Working Group on Child and Family Services

Information, 2002)] have low educational attainment, have difficulty finding work, are over-represented in lower paying jobs, are over-represented on social assistance and tend to lack life skills and social supports (Rutman, Barlow, Alusik, Hubberstey, and Brown, 2003). This emphasizes the importance of having reliable outcome measures in child welfare and comparing these with outcomes for children in the general population.

7. Workload pressures

It was reported earlier that child welfare workers might be spending an inordinate amount time investigating referrals that are not appropriate for child protection services. Low risk families are typically "screened out" but many referrals still require workers to complete a safety assessment before making a decision to close the case. This may be diverting staff time away from those families most in need.

Workers in most jurisdictions reported that there has been an increase in the number of children and families with complex needs coming to the attention of the child welfare system (Anderson & Goeil, 2003). This demands a level of intensive casework involvement that may not be possible with existing caseloads. In many instances, workers are able to provide little more than protective oversight for the families and children on their caseload. In a "better safe than sorry" environment, these children may be spending longer periods of time in care than necessary.

In an effort to improve accountability, many child welfare agencies have increased their administrative requirements (e.g., service standards, recording, financial reporting, information sharing protocols). While laudable from an accountability perspective, this may increase the demands on worker time and result in less time being available for direct contact with families.

There is evidence that an important source of caseload growth in child welfare can be attributed to families already known to the system. Over two thirds of investigations documented by the CIS were "re-openings." This includes cases closed after the child safety concerns were addressed but situations in which underlying family needs remain unmet. Low risk families that are initially screened out may also return to the system.

8. Scope of mandate and access to resources

There is little doubt that, after experiencing years of funding restraint throughout the 1990s and with the loss of transfer payments under the CHST, provinces have simply been unable to provide child welfare systems with the resource base to respond to the multiple, complex, and varying needs of families. Yet, there are many different types of support services that exist around child welfare. Many of these services that could be available to support families in stressful situations are under separate governance structures with distinct service systems. As a result, it may be difficult for child welfare staff to access these services in an efficient manner.

In addition to the more formal services like schools, health, day care, and home visitor programs, there are many informal community based supports that, if utilized effectively, could divert families away from the child protection system. It may be these informal supports that offer the greatest potential to build social networks around parents under stress. Unfortunately, it has been difficult to mobilize these informal resources due to case specific workload demands on staff and the adversarial nature of child protection work.

What can be done? A new approach to child welfare

Child welfare continues to be somewhat of an enigma to governments and their senior administrators. Despite the legislative changes, the number of children in care continues to increase and child welfare budgets have proven to be almost impossible to control. Further, there is a dearth of convincing information to show that child welfare is being effective in protecting children at risk or successful in raising children into adulthood. The findings of recent studies are challenging some of the traditional assumptions upon which contemporary child welfare systems have been structured. What can be done? What new strategies might work?

Without question, the most critical component of child welfare has proven to be the front end of the system, involving intake and investigation. If child welfare is going to become more effective, this is where the changes must occur. The solution might be found in a "narrowing plus" strategy. In this context, narrowing means clarifying the mandate of child welfare agencies and by doing so, ensuring that professional workers focus their time on working with high risk families. The plus part of this means finding ways for families whose cases might otherwise be closed at intake to obtain the supports they require.

Child welfare workers must be allowed to use their highly tuned investigative and assessment skills in appropriate circumstances. Families with significant child safety issues should receive a child protection response from a professional worker. Staff with the expertise in investigation, evidence gathering and the court process must be allowed to focus their work on high-risk cases. At the same time, there is no need to bring into the adversarial child welfare system families for whom there is no immediate child protection concern. These families should be provided with non-adversarial support to assist them to deal with stress and difficult circumstances. This has a preventive component and can help ensure these families do not return later as high risk cases.

The "narrowing plus" strategy could involve a dual response system where cases are streamed according to degree of risk and presenting needs. High risk cases would be referred to child protection while cases with no immediate safety concerns would be referred to a non-adversarial stream to be assessed for support services. For this to be successful, child welfare must find more effective ways to work with other systems in a more formalized and coordinated manner.

An effective alternate response system must be based on a broadened intake and screening system with formal linkages between child welfare and other service providers. With the removal of the CAP funding conditions, federal transfers are no longer in jeopardy if social services like child welfare are integrated with other systems such as education, health or youth corrections. Systems and different providers can more easily work in partnership at the front end to ensure that high risk families are referred to child welfare and other families are not left without supports.

Options for implementing this dual response strategy include:

- establishing a common governance structure to oversee multiple service providers;
- developing service contracts or formalized protocols where the contribution of other service providers to the overall goal of child welfare is clearly articulated; or
- creating integrated intake systems in which a variety of different providers are involved in the early responses to a referral.

Another approach that could have an impact on the front end of the system is to create a more prominent, important, and well-defined role for community based supports. This would require a concentrated mobilization strategy to build understanding at the community level that the welfare of children is everyone's responsibility. In order to build a meaningful role for community supports, there must be clarification of what child welfare can and should do. Communities must also have the resources to meet the needs of these families. All too often the lack of appropriate community services leads to referrals to child welfare: the service of last resort.

Child welfare must, directly or in partnership with other systems, work with local community groups to recruit and train volunteers to provide support services to families in stressful situations. Informal networks may be the best resource available to alleviate feelings of isolation and to help families deal with difficult situations that they encounter on a regular basis. The overriding goal is to create a capacity within local neighborhoods to provide supports as a way of diverting families away from child welfare. Examples include volunteers to provide emergency child care in crisis situations, visitors to reduce feelings of social isolation, and peer delivered parent education and peer counselling programs within a community resource centre model.

Given the findings of the first Canadian Incidence Study of Reported Child Abuse and Neglect, it is important that child welfare providers develop a capacity to respond to child neglect. Neglect is the single most cited reason for referrals and case openings, yet child welfare agencies may be ill equipped to deal with these circumstances. A flexible funding model is needed to allow child welfare authorities to use their resources in new and creative ways to more directly meet the basic needs of families. Other provincial programs like social assistance that can provide financial resources for families should have a more practical, formalized, and meaningful involvement with child welfare. This should be more that just a referral to the other service system. A formal partnership between child welfare and these other programs is essential.

Finally, where it is not possible to alleviate the protection concerns and a child does come into the care of the state, that child has a right to be expeditiously placed into a permanent family setting. The next placement for a child in care should be the last placement. Some jurisdictions have strengthened regulations requiring more timely and comprehensive permanency planning. Legislation at both the federal and state levels in the United States has stringent requirements for timely permanency planning for children in care. A national strategy for permanency planning should be developed. In addition to strict legislated timelines, a broad range of placement and reunification options needs to be developed to ensure that a permanent decision *that best meets the needs of each child* can be made in a timely fashion. A comprehensive and consistent approach to adoption of children in care should be part of this strategy. There has been much success in some jurisdictions in the United States in using services from private adoption agencies. Kinship adoptions based on growing kinship care practices should be examined. For older children who cannot be reunified with their parents, "open adoptions" need to be reconsidered to ensure that children who have maintained contact with their families can be adopted.

A new approach to child welfare: Next steps

Perhaps the most important resource available to governments, ministers of social services, and child welfare administrators is new information. If child welfare is going to evolve, it must begin to operate in a "learning environment," building on successes in different jurisdictions. Inter-provincial cooperation and regular discussions at the national level are critical to this success. Provincial governments should lobby the federal government to play a leadership role in the development and distribution of national data in the child welfare field.

There are particular information areas in Canada where some significant progress has already been made. The findings from studies such as the Canadian Incidence Study of Reported Child Abuse and Neglect are extremely informative and can support the planning process on a national level. The continued evolution of child welfare must be driven by sound knowledge and informed choices. Recent collaboration on outcome measures is also very encouraging in this regard. The advancement of best practice approaches should be influenced by strong evaluations of child welfare outcomes. It is necessary that child welfare administrators learn more about what does and does not work in this field.

In a national forum, provinces and territories should begin the process of clarifying the role and mandate of child protection services within the broader context of meeting the needs of families. As part of this process, provinces and territories should collaborate on a strategy to implement pilot projects across the country to assess whether the "narrowing plus" strategy can be effective. These pilot projects should include a community capacity building component to mobilize informal supports.

It is also critical that a national strategy on permanency planning and adoption be developed to ensure that children in care can transition to a family environment in a timely manner.

Whatever plans and new directions are designed for child welfare, Aboriginal representatives must be included in all discussions. Aboriginal leaders at both the national and provincial levels should be included as full partners in all national meetings to map out a strategy for child welfare.

Avenues for positive innovations in Canadian child welfare: Lessons from the Partnerships for Children and Families Project and international jurisdictions

Gary Cameron, Nancy Freymond, and Catherine Roy

Abstract

Child welfare in Canada has been shaped by dichotomized visions promoting either child protection or parent assistance, emphasizing the legal system or welfare services. In this chapter, authors argue that this child protection paradigm projects a false image of what is possible or desirable. Themes drawn from the experiences of parents and service providers participating in the Partnerships for Children and Families Project, a collaborative project involving universities, children's aid societies, children's mental health centres, and associations of parents, are presented. Descriptions of selected international positive systems of child and family welfare follow. Based on these data, avenues for positive innovations in Canadian child and family welfare are proposed. The discussion points to more acceptable reforms for parents and children that provide them a broader range of useful resources and allow direct service providers to spend most of their time helping families. The need for developing collaborative partnerships among informal and formal service providers is also highlighted.

Introduction

For the past one hundred years, "child saving" principles have provided the foundation for child welfare systems in Canada (Cameron, Freymond, Cornfield, & Palmer, 2001). Despite shifts in emphasis, from family preservation to investigation of families and apprehension of children, the dominant focuses remain protecting children from harm within their own homes, holding parents accountable for the "proper" care of their children, and removing children to more "appropriate" places to live. In addition, child welfare in Canada has been shaped by dichotomized visions promoting either the protection of children or assistance for parents, emphasizing the legal system or welfare services, focusing on state care of children or maintaining the viability of families, relying on central control or on local discretion. This "either/or" mentality projects a false image of what is possible and what is desirable.

Our belief is that this Canadian child protection paradigm has very little potential to help children and parents that we have not already seen. One of our basic tenets is that the capacity to respond to the complexities facing children and families is unnecessarily limited by what the paradigm allows us to see and to try. Another is that any serious search for improvements in child welfare outcomes must examine multiple aspects of the delivery system and resist the politically expedient, but ultimately impractical, temptation of single solutions.

Ontario's child welfare system recently made a substantial shift towards legalism and central control through prescribed procedures and time-lines for interventions with families. Changes emphasize formal risk assessment and the investigation and oversight of families. As a result, the number of families eligible for investigation and the number of children in state care have increased dramatically under modified mandatory reporting guidelines and new obligations to investigate. The cost of maintaining Ontario's children's aid societies has more than doubled over the past six years; yet 50 of 52 societies projected a budget deficit in the 2001-02 fiscal year ("Ontario's children's," 2003). Despite these societies having access to more financial resources than ever before, their front-line service providers feel overwhelmed by accountability and legal procedures and discouraged by their inability to spend sufficient time with families (Cameron, Freymond, et al., 2001; Regehr, Leslie, Howe, & Chau, 2000). Increasing numbers of workers fear the legal consequences should a tragedy occur with one of their cases. Recruiting and retaining qualified staff is also a continuing challenge (Coulthard et al., 2001).

This chapter extrapolates lessons for reform from the experiences of families and service providers involved with Ontario's children's aid societies and identifies opportunities for positive innovations in Canadian child welfare systems drawing upon selected international jurisdictions. Information from the continuing program of research and development at the Partnerships for Children and Families Project[1] made these analyses

---

1 The Partnerships for Children and Families Project is a five-year (2000–2005) Community University Research Alliance funded by the Social Sciences and Humanities Research Council of Canada. It involves researchers from Wilfrid Laurier, Guelph and McMaster universities. Community partners include four children's aid societies, three children's mental health centres and two associations of parents involved with these services in south central Ontario.

possible. Specifically, this chapter draws upon 180 qualitative interviews,[2] 16 parent and service provider focus groups, and 504 service provider survey questionnaires completed during the first phase of the Partnership Project research. The authors highlight a purposeful selection of themes that emerged from the interviews with parents and service providers. We then discuss illustrations from selected international positive systems of child and family welfare. In both sections, avenues for positive innovations in Canadian child and family welfare are highlighted.

The lives of parents and families

Understanding the daily living realities and service experiences of children and parents involved with child welfare and residential children's mental health services is a primary focus of the Partnerships Project research. Most of the following case illustrations come from life story interviews with 16 mothers and interviews with 30 mothers who had a child placed outside the family home by a child welfare agency.

Stereotypes

Prejudices about the parents involved with children's aid societies are virulent. There is little public sympathy for who we imagine these people to be and a strong predilection to judge and to punish. Two feature articles in the Kitchener-Waterloo Record (Etherington, 2000a, 2000b) display a portrait of families that is unsympathetic and offers little hope for positive change:

> "…four hungry kids under the age of six… surrounded by guns, crack and cocaine while their grandmother sold stolen property…."

> "…the baby boy had 15 fractured ribs, two skull fractures, hemorrhaging in his eyes, a broken collar bone and a spinal injury… had been severely shaken and had his head smashed against the wall by teenage parents…."

> "…the Kitchener father was forcing his teenage son to take part in anal and oral sex …."

> "… found a baby and a young boy in a vermin-infested house … contacted by hospital staff who had treated the kids' mother for rat bites … found the children in a bedroom surrounded by animal feces and dead mice …."

---

2   These include life story interviews, family interviews, and co-authorship interviews with parents, as well as individual interviews with parents and service providers.

While such extreme family circumstances are seen by child welfare workers, these portraits are so removed from the lives of almost all of the families in our investigations, including families who've had a child placed in state care, to be both misleading and prejudicial. In addition, these public portraits serve to convince the reader that child protection services must act with firm authority with such families. On the other hand, the contrasting portraits presented below lead us to ask: Who benefits from such an unbalanced characterization of families involved with child welfare?

Overcoming

The extraordinary number, duration and intensity of the challenges that mothers involved with child welfare services encounter in their lives is a common theme that emerged from our research. Yet these women's stories were not of unremitting woe and helplessness. Painful difficulties continued, but there were present joys and hopes for the future in many of these stories. These women understood their lives in terms of their continuing effort and their persistence and their desire and capacity to do better, attributes that are not adequately acknowledged in our images of mothers nor in our helping strategies in child welfare:

> **Skylar:**[3] "It's just a bunch of hurdles…. There's still probably going to be a thousand more hurdles in my life. So I'll still get over them, just like an Olympic athlete or something."
>
> **Annette:** "I'm a never giver upper. I'm determined that everybody around me is going to be happy, including myself … the movie of my life would be how rough it was at the start and how beautiful it is at the end."

Life opportunities and the pressures of daily living

There were no affluent families in our research, and very few could satisfy conventional criteria for a "middle class" life. But contrary to the public stereotype of "lazy" parents, our data highlight the extraordinary pressures on mothers as many worked outside the home and tried to hold families together. In addition, quite a few of the older mothers talked about returning to complete high school and sometimes to attend college as adults.

While it is well known that child welfare in many jurisdictions focuses its

---

3   The names of individuals are fictitious to protect their identities while allowing a range of different stories to be presented.

attention primarily on disadvantaged families (Courtney, 1998; English, 1998), in our research, this general reality affected neither assessments of family situations nor helping strategies, which remained focused on modifying parental behaviours. The unavoidable reality is that, whether we concentrate on protecting children from specific types of harm or on improving their well-being, these are the socio-economic environments that almost all of the children involved with child welfare grow up in. However, the child protection interventions in our research were not particularly congruent with the day to day needs and expectations of these children **nor** their parents:

> *Amber:* "I put myself back in school because I only made it to grade eight and I figured I'm not going to get anywhere in life…. And it took me almost six years… to get my Grade 12 and I have a learning disability…."
>
> *Susan:* "Thinking back… I don't know how we even managed. …during the summer we were having a hard time paying the bills and so… twice the bill was late and it [hydro] was up for disconnection when I'd go down and pay it… if we don't have hydro we have no food, no nothing, right."

Mothers' personal struggles

It is mothers' histories, attitudes and behaviours that are most under scrutiny in child protection (Swift, 1995). In our research, mothers undertook, and were expected to undertake, a disproportionate share of the burden of bringing about requested changes in family life. Many of the mothers had disrupted and painful journeys in their childhoods, and in their adult lives. Unstable childhoods and living on their own at a very young age were common, as were experiences of childhood maltreatment or domestic violence. Anecdotes of addictions, particularly alcohol abuse, were in many stories, most commonly in childhood homes and with male partners, but sometimes in mothers' own struggles with addictions. A minority of mothers talked about ongoing physical or emotional health problems.

Portraits of the personal difficulties and limitations of mothers involved with child welfare are common (Bagely & Young, 1999; Harden, 1998; Woodward & Fergusson, 2002). Corroborating this emphasis, each of the child welfare service provider focus groups reading a selection of these women's stories initially focused on the "unresolved personal issues" of these women. Yet, none of the women in these stories had the resources nor the time to invest in lengthy programs of personal recovery. A question raised by the research team is: "What claim did these women have upon our compassion and helping efforts, independent of the needs of their children?" The evidence indicates that compassion for mothers is not in ample supply in child welfare in Ontario these days:

> *Amy:* "My mom was a single parent… until I was 11 so it was pretty tough. My mom had a lot of… substance abuse problems…. We didn't know she had bi-polar and she would get very, very angry and physically abusive…. When I was first born, they took me away from my mother for two years because she was an unfit mother…."

> *Amber:* "I come from a very… rough background. …a lot of fights in the family a lot of abuse… [Amber's father] was a pretty abusive man. I go to counseling for it and my head's still screwed up…. He hit me in the face and I went through most of my life… hiding behind… drugs, alcohol, just blocking it out. I bounced around a lot when I was a kid. After they broke up, I was in foster homes, grandmother, aunts, uncles… I'm full blooded. I've always looked highly on it."

The struggles and continuity of family

In light of the personal challenges and the family life difficulties facing many of these mothers, it is easy to understand why child protection authorities might be concerned about their children and why many of these women appreciated positive assistance with these problems. While a minority of these women were in stable, long-term marriages, most described a series of quite troubled relationships with male partners over time. Most of the children in these stories were not living with their biological fathers and, in many families, siblings had different biological fathers. A relatively small proportion of stories revealed physical or sexual mistreatment of children as the reason for official child welfare concern.

Such problems in family functioning have been a predominant focus of the discussions in child welfare for many years (Karen, 1990; Kline & Overstreet, 1972; Ratiner, 2000). What is almost completely absent from this established story is recognition of the continuity and central place of family in the lives of these mothers and children. Most of these mothers strongly desired a stable home for themselves and their children. Despite past difficulties, the incentive to have a positive partner relationship was strong and most of the women connected with a new partner who often was considered an important source of support. A significant pattern was the pivotal importance of members of extended families in the lives of at least half of these mothers. Most unexpected was the finding that, for many women, their own mother had become an important source of emotional and social support in their adult lives, sometimes in spite of horrendous experiences as children. Not all mothers saw their parents or extended families as helpful. Yet, some mothers without access to such support expressed their longing to belong and for someone to care.

These are not only mothers and families with limitations. These stories also illustrate the persistence, commitment and capacities of many of these mothers and these families. These are capacities that the Canadian child protection paradigm is particularly ill suited to recognize and to strengthen. Pressure on individual mothers and families to change is a grossly insufficient model of helping. Not withstanding that coercive authority is required in some situations, and that difficulties often appear overwhelming, a root challenge in improving outcomes in Canadian child welfare is connecting to these shared realities in ways that provide more resources and that build upon the motivation and talents apparent in these life stories:

> **Karen:** "…both Jeremy and Trevor [Karen's boys] they were the best experience. Like they were the best experience…. Bill [Trevor's dad] wasn't into… family life… he didn't want to be involved anymore…. He started getting a lot more aggressive… he went into drinking, doing drugs, hanging out with his friends…. I stayed at the shelter for a couple of months… he was actually arrested…. And that's when the children's aid had come into my life… [current partner] been sort of a friend to me… he's a really good person… a very responsible person. And he's good to me. …he loves us and I love him, and the kids love him… we get along so well…."

> **Elizabeth:** "…I'm a mom and I try to do my best to work things out… now I've learned to deal with things in other ways besides turning to alcohol and drugs… my attentions are more focused on my children… because I've done a lot of counseling and self help things…."

Child welfare services

While mothers in our study were very aware of difficulties in their homes, many of them were quite confused about the exact nature of child welfare concerns about their families and what was expected of them. Unifying themes of their experiences with child welfare were fear, mistrust and, at best, ambivalence about its value. First contact with a child protection worker was a particularly frightening experience for many mothers.

Nonetheless, woven through many stories were anecdotes of appreciated help. Despite most mothers meeting several service providers while their case was open, and commenting about the lack of credibility of young workers who've not had children of their own, some mothers talked about individual child protection workers from whom they felt understanding and "extra" efforts to be supportive. For many, child protection involvement did lead to willing or "coerced" changes in parenting practices and was instrumental in reducing levels of partner conflict and violence in homes, at least in the short term.

Despite these benefits, the overall tone of these stories is of mothers "doing whatever is necessary" and "waiting for Children's Aid to leave." Mothers' most prevalent critique was that, even when they were looking for help, they had surprisingly little face-to-face or telephone contact with child welfare service providers, including while under supervision orders for "high risk" home conditions. Another frustration for some mothers was not seeing anyone from the child welfare agency after their child was returned home from care.

Equally clear in these stories was that most families, regardless of the variations in their circumstances, were the focus of a limited standard set of expectations from child welfare: attend various types of counseling, go to 12-step programs and addictions treatment, attend anger management groups, take a parenting course, make changes in housing conditions and improve relations in the home. Typically, mothers felt "told" rather than supported to do these things; few had any illusions about the consequences of non-compliance. Also striking was the general absence in these stories of helping interventions focused on children, beyond periodic referrals for counseling. For the research team, direct assistance to children emerged as a promising and practical area for improvements in how we choose to protect children and to promote the well-being of children and their families:

> *Sky:* "They're like 'can we sit down?' I'm like 'fine.' And I get in hysterics. I should have stayed calm but I couldn't. They kinda just sat down and start throwing questions at you…you have no chance to just know what they're saying, cause they sound like chipmunks… everything's in fast. So, I was like 'what are you talking about?'… Like the first minute they walk in the door, you can't breathe… and then before you know it, your whole life's gone."
>
> *Karen:* "'Cause I'd heard so many horror stories… I could have said no to them… I don't need any help… I was worried… I thought, they're in your house, and they're gonna have some

kind of… a warrant…. I felt like I had no other choice… Debbie, my worker, she's been really nice. She's been super nice. …they did provide… a lot of programs… introduced me to a lot of things… I don't feel like there was such a … priority for them to come into my life… maybe I needed that step to actually get my… ex out of my life."

Most of the apprehended children in our study returned home, sometimes after a relatively short time in care. For the research team, the use of child apprehension as a precaution or as leverage for family change emerged as a priority niche for the development of more constructive alternatives. For mothers, these were truly horrible experiences and, in their eyes, frightening for their children:

Annette: "…then the children's aid society guy goes, 'we're leaving right now.' That was all that was said… there he was walking out with both my children, and I lost it. I went down on my knees, I screamed, I yelled, I done everything…. I was just trembling…. Five days later, my children were dropped off at the shelter. Right after court, I went right to the shelter and I met my children there."

Jennifer: "When they took Rachael, [her daughter] it really hurt my grandparents because we live with them…. All they did was cry every day… [The night Children's Aid removed her daughter]… a woman cop… whispered to me that I'd better agree and do what the children's services said or I'll never see my kid again…."

Information from child welfare service providers about child welfare services did not paint a very different picture from the mothers' versions. It was quite common for service providers to indicate that they were the third or even the fourth person assigned to the case since it had been open. Between 69% to 71% of direct service workers in three children's aid societies estimated that they spend less than 35% of their time working with families. Indeed, in two of these agencies, 40% to 50% of direct service workers believed that they spent less than 20% of their time contacting families. Most spent the majority of their time satisfying the legal and procedural recording requirements of their job. Given the magnitude of the challenges facing the families in this study, and the seriousness of the decisions made by child protection workers, it is disturbing how little familiarity these service providers had with these families and how little time they had available to help.

Focus groups with service providers

In our focus group interviews, service providers illustrated the distance between their employment realities and mothers' experiences. Disconcerting examples included disparaging remarks about mothers' capacities to understand themselves or their relationships and their potential to do better in the future. These data highlight the major barriers in current child protection arrangements to establishing knowing and trusting helping relationships between mothers and child welfare service providers. A dramatic concern is that about half of the direct service workers indicated very high levels of emotional exhaustion on the Maslach Burnout Inventory scale for emotional exhaustion (Maslach & Jackson, 1986). Many direct service providers questionned their ability to do their jobs as they thought they should be done in the time available. A paradoxical image was that a substantial majority of direct service providers were, overall, moderately or highly satisfied with their job, including its intellectual challenge, its financial rewards and the organizational support that they received in their work. In the focus groups, service providers emphasized the importance of the work that they were trying to do.

For the authors, these contrasting images of working in child welfare suggest that the systemic difficulties which emerged in these analyses are not substantially attributable to the financial resources available to these children's aid societies nor to the quality of management support in these agencies. Our contention is that they are endemic in how the Ontario child protection paradigm understands and implements the "protection" of children.

Our research portrays an expensive and inefficient child welfare system which does not provide children or parents with notable levels of useful assistance nor create a coherent mandate for service providers. Three areas for system innovation emerge from these analyses: (1) developing enriched and flexible first response systems; (2) making available to children and parents a much broader repertoire of useful resources, and; (3) engaging a substantially higher proportion of parents and children in helping efforts that they find acceptable.

Selected niches for innovation in Canadian child welfare

Enriched and flexible first responses

In the 1990s, several American states implemented pilot differential response models. A differential response model limits investigative responses to urgent or high risk situations, while assessment and support services are offered in family circumstances considered less "threatening" to children. In a differential response assessment system, workers are expected to assess needs and to provide resources based on a customized response for each family (Waldfogel, 2001b). Although differential response models have the potential for multiple tracks of service delivery, most states developed dual track response systems (Trocmé, Knott, & Roy, 2003).

From our perspective, the rift in the Anglo American child protection paradigm between protecting children and supporting families predisposes proponents towards a bifurcated system of first responses. The separation of care and control functions into distinct delivery systems led to a debate over the classification of referrals into those who merit assessment and community intervention and those who require investigation and standard protection interventions. Another design option is to develop a first response system that maintains a constructive flow of involvements between units with supportive mandates and those with investigative mandates. Many families who enter child welfare systems can benefit from a mixture of compassionate and authoritative assistance (Cameron, Freymond, et al., 2001). Ideally, to be effective, differential response models require extensive community partnerships where child protection agencies "play the lead role" but share responsibility with community service providers to protect children (Waldfogel, 2001b).

Such an emphasis on creating community partnerships for child protection agencies is, in large part, not a central concern in many European countries, where the child welfare mandate has historically been shared across multiple partners in the social welfare and youth justice systems. For example, it is common in several European nations for local generic service organizations to provide assistance to distressed families and to be the first contact with many families suspected of maltreatment.

> In Finland, the child welfare legislation reforms of 1990 emphasise preventive, non-stigmatising, and supportive measures and services. One of the central objectives of the reform was to shift the emphasis of child welfare from extra familial care to measures that encourage and support the maintenance of children in their own home. As a result, work methods of all welfare services, were adapted toward strengthening child rearing by carers. Maternity and child health clinics have expanded and diversified family training, and intensified co-operation with families. In day care, various forms of co-operation supporting parental par-

ticipation were developed. Also home help services have been developed to support child rearing by parents. (Tuomisto & Vuori-Karvia, 1997, p. 92)

The co-location of various services in neighborhood settings has proved to be important in expanding the role of community agencies in differential response models of child welfare. This co-location of services is also convenient for families. Schene (2002) argues that co-location facilitates the coordination of interventions, supports relationship building between professionals and indigenous community leaders, and allows professionals to develop an understanding of the community in which they work (Schene, 2002). Clearly, for a differential response approach to be of real value to children, parents and families, there has to be a richness of formal and informal helping and community involvement resources available.

An expanded range of "family friendly" child placement options

In our research, there was a clear pattern of apprehending children temporarily while parental capacity is evaluated and using "heightened" parental motivation during care to secure changes in family functioning. For the substantial majority of families in which children will not be out of their homes a long time, our research advocates strongly for the development of alternative procedures with a capacity both to reassure service providers and to be acceptable to parents and children.

One choice is to develop a system of supportive and flexible placement options allowing service providers more alternatives to respond to individual family circumstances. A practical consideration of this proposal is that it draws on resources and abilities existing in children's aid societies. Continuity in the parent-child relationship is possible when placements are available for parents and children together. For young mothers, a supportive placement with an experienced mother may improve the parent-child relationship. Our research also suggests the value of having access to short term parent-child placements in situations of family violence when shelter space is not available immediately.

Sweden uses placements in small public institutions called homes for care and accommodation. These homes generally accommodate nine or fewer children from birth to 12 years. Andersson (2002) indicates that 90% of these homes admit children and parents together. During the placement period, the capacity of the family is assessed and a plan established for ongoing support to the family upon return home or for the placement of the child in ongoing foster care. Another "popular" Swedish intervention is establishing a relationship between a contact family/person and a family where child maltreatment is a concern. This family-to-family relationship provides non-professional support to children and families. Children may also stay over with a contact person/family for a short time if needed. A local social welfare committee appoints the contact family/person, often after an assessment of the needs of the child and the family.

Many countries report an increased emphasis on placement with members of extended families in the past decade, most notably in the USA (O'Brien, 2001). In Canadian substitute care, using families' social networks or extended families as placement options has not been emphasized. Yet, placing children within social networks and extended families members has many advantages. During a crisis, the placement of a child with someone who is known and trusted by the child reduces anxiety for all family members. The foster parents and the biological parents may have a history enabling continuity for the child, as well as natural opportunities for connections between parents and children and between the two families. Iglehart (1994) provides evidence that children who are placed with relatives have lower rates of disruption and adjust better to placement experiences. Also, placing children within social networks and extended families helps to preserve both individual and cultural identities and feelings of belonging.

Access to expanded and flexible support placement options allows greater tailoring of interventions to the specific family conditions. Equally important, our research stresses the importance of reducing "unnecessarily cruel" placement experiences for mothers and children and expanding the space where parents and service providers can agree about what is to be done. For example, in many European countries most child placements result from negotiated agreements with parents rather than from formal court orders (Cameron, Freymond, et al., 2001).

Increased space for consensual and negotiated agreements

Our research shows that direct service workers in Ontario's children's aid societies spend much of their time satisfying the requirements for evidence of the formal legal system. In Ontario's child protection system, service providers manage their concerns about child safety, and their doubts about parental capacity, by relying on the authority of the courts. Also, in the current political climate, child welfare service providers have strong incentives to secure court orders to protect themselves against civil and criminal liability should a tragedy occur. An essential precursor to providing more helpful resources to families, and a less conflicted environment for service providers, is to greatly reduce the proportion of families in which a formal legal application for a supervision order or the placement of a child is necessary. In our research, direct service workers described a loss of confidence emanating from their reliance on court authority to justify their involvement with families.

Hetherington, Cooper, Smith, & Wilford (1997) propose broadening the intermediary space between the role of supporting families and the role of the law in child welfare. Without spaces where agreements can be negotiated, child welfare service providers' work is inevitably procedural in nature and limited substantially to being an agent of state control (King, 1995). In intermediary spaces, "everyone—children, parents, professionals—finds room to think, negotiate, plan, in the middle of the intensely complex and often long-term process of working out optimum solutions in cases of child abuse" (Hetherington et al., 1997, p. 7).

The inclusion of such intermediary space requires a repositioning of legal services and courts to ancillary positions in Canadian child welfare. Judicial orders would be reserved for situations of immediate and serious risk to children or when efforts to secure parental cooperation have failed. Negotiated or mediated agreements would become the norm and coercive court applications used in emergencies or as a last resort. This opens possibilities for direct service workers to ascertain families' needs and preferences, to negotiate helping and child protection strategies, and to develop constructive helping relationships with family members. In situations where direct service workers cannot reach agreement with families on their own, an increased access to mediation services would be appropriate. Mediation services have been on the fringes of child welfare in Ontario for years. They have demonstrated a potential to achieve negotiated agreements and to preserve positive helping relationships (Maresca, 1995; McNeilly, 1997; Hetherington et al., 1997).

Some European systems,[4] such as those of France and Belgium, make frequent use of the authority of family judges (often specially trained for this purpose) in a less formal fashion in negotiating intervention plans with families and service providers. Other jurisdictions such as Finland, Flemish Belgium, Germany, and Denmark also have legislated informal negotia-

---

4 The information about European experiences with intermediary negotiating spaces is used with permission from Cameron, Freymond, et al., 2001.

tions with families to resolve concerns about the care of children. This legislation is based on the principle that assistance to families should be framed as an offer of help, rather than as a command from a legal authority; the intent is to offer parents some freedom of choice about their families and to foster a feeling of self-help, rather than control (Bering Pruzan, 1997; Wolff, 1997).

Belgium's Flemish community makes extensive use of mediation in child welfare. When the voluntary relationship between service providers and the family breaks down, when attempts to secure family "cooperation" prove futile, or when voluntary services are not producing the desired family "change," mediation becomes mandatory. Luckock and colleagues (1997) questioned whether a volunteer committee can grasp the dynamics in abusive families. However, these mediation committees have no authority beyond attempting to bring about a voluntary, mutually agreeable helping agreement between social workers and families. If there is a failure to reach agreement, the committee refers the family, via the public prosecutor, to the Judge for Children.

The Scottish Children's Hearing, conducted by a panel composed of three lay members who are appointed and work on a voluntary basis, is unique within the United Kingdom (King, 1995). The Children's Panel is concerned with the welfare of the child and does not deal with cases where there are disputes over the facts. There are legal grounds for referral to a panel, when the parents and the child (when the child has the capacity to understand) agree, before the hearing proceeds. If there is no agreement on the legal grounds, the case goes to the Sheriff's Court. After the grounds are established, the case returns for a Children's Hearing. The child, the parents, the reporter, and the social worker attend this meeting with the panel, after which a plan for the care of the child is developed. In situations where immediate protection is required, an emergency court order may be sought, which is a temporary measure until longer-term solutions are arranged (King, 1995).

Deciding to use community volunteers or to employ professional mediators is reflective of the position of child welfare services in relation to the broader community. Societies where the well-being of children is understood as a collective responsibility may be more inclined to use community volunteers. In either instance, mediation processes should be publicly known so that child welfare service providers, parents and older children understand that they have a right to ask for mediation assistance.

A different variant of intermediate space, where negotiations between the family members, service workers, and a Judge for Children take place, occurs in several European jurisdictions. This form of "informal negotiating" happens in societies with "inquisitorial" legal systems. This tradition allows judges to take a more active role in asking questions and gathering information than is allowed in "adversarial" legal systems, such as Canada's. In such situations, fewer cases go to contested court hearings and most service decisions—even those involving the placement of a child—occur with the agreement of parents.

In France, such intermediary procedures are introduced, usually before more coercive, legal action is taken. Families reportedly can and do make use of the Judge for Children's office to receive assistance and referrals. Hetherington and her colleagues (1997) note that:

> ...the process of the hearing is informal and the family is in direct discussion with the judge... By law, the judge has to attempt to get the agreement of the parents to any order he makes and failure to do this can be the grounds for appeal. (p. 65)

Judges in "Anglo-American" child protection systems would not see many of the cases that come before French judges, either because the families would not have met the criteria for child protection services or there would not have been sufficient evidence to take the families to court. In contrast, "French participants estimate that only about 10% of the cases that come before Judges for Children involve maltreatment" (Pires, 1993, p. 46).

Similarly, the inquisitorial courts in Germany provide an intermediary structure for families in the child welfare system. The German courts operate on the principle of voluntary jurisdiction:

> Parties can be represented and witnesses can be heard but the judge holds sole responsibility for the investigation.... Judges have a mediating as well as an investigative function and will frequently conduct "round table" discussions which take into consideration all the provisions available under the KJHG [*Kinder und Jugendhilfegesetz* or Children and Youth Services Act] to help a child and its family. (Wilford, Hetherington & Piquardt, 1997, p. 18–19)

German families are normally involved in all decisions concerning their welfare, especially when developing a plan of action in cases of crisis or need (Wilford et al., 1997). However, in cases of extreme severity, or when agreements cannot be reached, interventions for families can be legally mandated (Wolff, 1997).

A Canadian variant exists in British Columbia where the Child, Family and Community Service Act provides judicial processes designed to avoid contested applications to the courts. A judicial case conference is mandatory in new apprehensions and acts as "the gateway for future process toward the ultimate decisions for the benefit of the child by the parents, social workers, Aboriginal bands or the judge" (Schmidt, 2001, p. 3). Judges engage parents and social workers in discussion for the purposes of resolving disputes. A case conference does not address whether a child is "in need of protection," but may order temporary or continuing care in an effort to keep the focus on the needs of the child, rather than the faults of the caregiver (Schmidt, 2001). Judges may make any order that the parties agree to, refer particular issues to community mediators, or make recommendations or orders that move the case to a formal hearing. In the urban centres of Surrey, Vancouver and Victoria, approximately 26% of cases that have case conferences proceed to trial (Schmidt, 2001).

Conclusion

Evidence in this chapter confirms that, for many mothers, involvement with Ontario's child protection system is an unwelcome, frightening, and, too often, marginally useful experience. For direct service workers, children's aid societies' mandate create a tension between the perceived importance of their work and their capacity to do the work as they believe it should be done. We argue for reforms that are more acceptable to parents and children, provide a broader range of useful resources to parents and children, and allow more direct service providers to spend most of their time helping children and their families.

This discussion points to a need for the development of collaboration with informal and formal partners to expand and to share the mandate for the protection of children and the support of families. However, we also highlight the importance of reforms within mandated child protection agencies both to reduce contradictions for direct service workers and to free scarce resources for other uses.

Others have argued for the timeliness of Canadian child welfare delivery system or service organization experiments (Cameron, Karabanow, Peirson, Laurendeau, & Chamberland, 2001). Such demonstrations offer a practical strategy for proceeding in light of strong resistance by established systems as well as a lack of familiarity with the complex requirements of the proposed reforms. The resources and infrastructures in place in some Ontario communities provide excellent venues for these types of experiments.

There are many neighbourhoods in Canada that have made extensive progress in the building of active partnerships among service organizations, including, in some cases, the local child protection agency. Also, many Canadian communities have made extensive gains in empowering local residents and developing an increased community capacity to respond to its own challenges. For example, most of the demonstration neighbourhoods in the Better Beginnings, Better Futures Primary Prevention Project in Cornwall, Regents Park, Kingston, Ottawa, Etobicoke, Sudbury and the Onward Willow community in Guelph have made exemplary gains, to varying degrees, in creating partnerships among service providers as well as local residents and professional helpers, and in empowering local neighbourhood leadership (Cameron & Cadell, 1999; Cameron, Hayward, McKenzie, Hancock, & Jeffery, 1999; Pancer & Cameron, 1994). What is missing for these communities, and their children's aid societies, is the possibility of relief from existing child protection legislative and funding constraints. In addition, any successful demonstration projects must have dependable project mandates, informed developmental guidance, and powerful and persistent official support. In any forthcoming innovations or experiments, it is important to keep in mind that there are no realistic quick or simple "solutions" to reforming Canadian child welfare and it remains essential to resist the siren call of the next "magic bullet."

Re-involving the community: The need for a differential response to rising child welfare caseloads in Canada

Nico Trocmé and Claire Chamberland

Abstract

This chapter describes the increase in child welfare caseloads that has been observed in Canada over the last decade. The authors argue that the current increase in investigations and children in need of protection provides an incomplete picture of the changes that have been occurring over a longer period of time. Data from the 1993 and 1998 Ontario incidence studies of reported child abuse and neglect are highlighted to provide a more detailed breakdown of some of the factors underlying these increases. A careful analysis of the data suggests the increases have not been uniform across all types of maltreatment. A detailed analysis of trends specific to types and severity of maltreatment as well as potential harm to children is also presented. In the second section, the authors argue for a broader array of intervention and prevention strategies that move beyond the actual child welfare system to mobilize community based services and supports. Challenges and benefits associated with alternative strategies are discussed. Potential benefits include improved partnerships among families, communities, and service providers; continuity of services; the assessment of children's needs rather than risks; and increased access to preventive services for vulnerable children and families.

Increasing caseloads across Canada

Child welfare caseloads have been increasing across Canada. Between 1996 and 2000, the number of child protection investigations increased 13% in British Columbia, 21% in Alberta and 55% in Quebec. Between 1993 and 1998, rates of investigated child abuse and neglect increased 44% while the number of substantiated cases doubled (Trocmé, Fallon, MacLaurin, & Copp, 2002). The number of children in care has been increasing as well in

Community collaboration and differential response:
Canadian and international research and emerging models of practice

Nico Trocmé, Della Knoke, and Catherine Roy, editors

"The greatest strength of this book is its overview of the major issues confronting those working for the well-being and protection of children. Its second great strength is the illustration of various emerging models in Canada and elsewhere that focus on the one key element required to improve the situation for children: community collaboration and participation. May this book inspire and support the efforts of everyone working for a more promising future for children and their families."

—**Jean-Marc Potvin**, *Director of Youth Protection Centre jeunesse de Montréal—Institut universitaire*

"The need for child welfare services that involve the community, that build on the strengths of families and communities, and that recognize the interdependence of formal and informal community partners in supporting families and car-

Part 1: Research and policy

- New directions in child welfare *Provincial and Territorial Directors of Child Welfare, with editing by Jay Rodgers*
- Avenues for positive innovations in Canadian child welfare: Lessons from the Partnerships for Children and Families Project and international jurisdictions *Gary Cameron, Nancy Freymond, and Catherine Roy*
- Re-involving the community: The need for a differential response to rising child welfare caseloads in Canada *Nico Trocmé and Claire Chamberland*
- Evaluating the implementation of assessment tools

Community collaboration and differential response:

Canadian and international research and emerging models of practice

Nico Trocmé, Della Knoke, and Catherine Roy, editors

Number of copies: _____ @ $30 Cdn (US$25) (Price includes shipping)

TOTAL = $ _____

_____
NAME

_____
ORGANIZATION

Order Form

some provinces. Between 1996 and 2002, the number of children in care increased 38% in British Columbia, 59% in Alberta, and 60% in Ontario. Between 1995 and 2001, the number of children from First Nations communities placed in out of home care increased by 71%.

These increases come in the wake of inquires into the tragic deaths of children who had been under the supervision of child welfare authorities. From the Gove inquiry in British Columbia to a series of six coroner's inquests in Ontario, to the Beaumont inquiry in Quebec, public pressure, new policy directives, and legislative changes had been calling for earlier and more decisive interventions. The pendulum having just swung away from "family centred" models towards more intrusive "child centred" models, service providers and policy makers are now wondering whether the pendulum should swing back.

The analogy of a pendulum swinging between family centred and child centred approaches to child welfare practice is well accepted, but in our opinion, poses a false dilemma that confuses issues. Child welfare policy and practice debates have tended to take place around poorly defined one-dimensional models: more intrusive vs. less intrusive; low risk vs. high risk; children's rights vs. parent's rights. The focus on crude indicators, such as caseloads and children in care, fails to recognize the complexity and diversity of need among children and families receiving child welfare services. Through a more detailed analysis of trends specific to different types of maltreatment and to different types of harm, we argue for a broader array of intervention and prevention strategies that move beyond the child welfare system to mobilize community based services and supports.

A 31-year perspective: Ontario, 1971-2002

The current increase in investigations and number of children in care provides an incomplete picture of the important changes that have been occurring over the longer term. Figure 1 tracks two important trends in Ontario over the past 30 years: the number of families served during the year and the number of children in care at year-end. Three distinct trends appear over this period of time with respect to children in care: (1) from the early 1970s to the mid-1980s, a sharp decrease in children in care corresponding to the dual impact of permanency planning and the decreased availability of foster homes; (2) from the mid-1980s to the mid-1990s, a period of relative stability; and (3) the recent increase in admissions to care.

Figure 1. Children in care and families served: Ontario 1971–2002

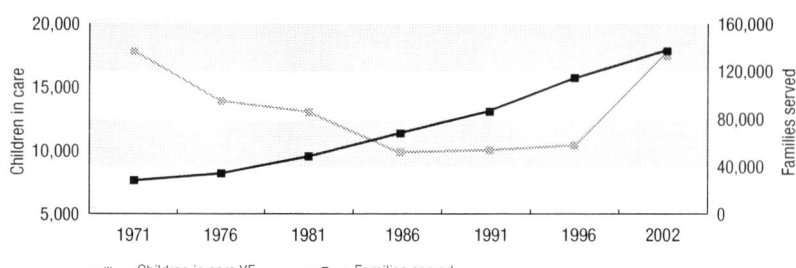

Throughout this period, the number of families served has increased at a fairly steady pace. As a result, the ratio of children in care to families served has dropped from 0.63 in 1971 to 0.09 in 1996, increasing slightly in the last few years to 0.13 in 2002. Service trends in most other Canadian jurisdictions appear to have followed a similar pattern. Although the recent increases in caseloads and admissions to care are indications of a potentially significant shift in approaches to child welfare practice across Canada, closer analysis is required to identify the factors driving these changes.

Differential trends by form of maltreatment: OIS 93-98

Two Ontario incidence studies of reported child abuse and neglect (OIS 1993 and OIS 1998) provide a more detailed breakdown of some of the factors underlying recent increases in investigation caseloads.[1] Between 1993 and 1998, the estimated number of child maltreatment investigations increased from 44,900 to 64,800 and the number of substantiated investigations nearly doubled, from 12,300 to 24,400.

Figure 2. Differential trends by form of maltreatment (OIS 93-98)

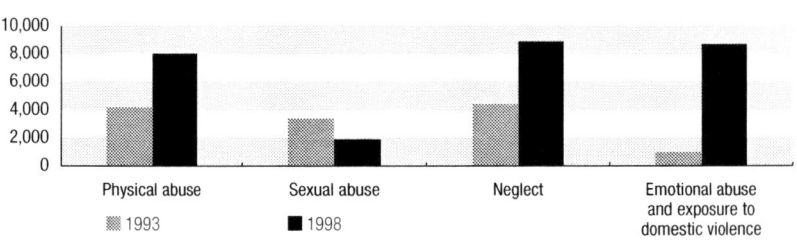

---

1 The *1998 Ontario Incidence Study of Reported Child Abuse and Neglect* (*OIS 1998*) is the most detailed source of child welfare investigation statistics available in Canada. The first *Canadian Incidence Study of Reported Child Abuse and Neglect* (*CIS 1998*) and the upcoming CIS 2003 will provide a similar level of detail across Canada.

The overall increase has not been uniform across types of maltreatment: rates of physical abuse have nearly doubled; rates of sexual abuse have decreased by 44%; rates of neglect have doubled; and rates of emotional maltreatment and exposure to domestic violence have increased nearly nine-fold (Trocmé, Fallon, MacLaurin, & Copp, 2002, Table 2a).

Physical abuse and corporal punishment

The number of substantiated investigations of physical abuse nearly doubled, growing from an estimated 4,200 in 1993 to 8,000 in 1998. Although physical abuse is often assumed to involve situations in which children have been severely harmed, in 55% of cases no physical harm was noted and severe harm requiring medical treatment was noted in only 6% of substantiated physical abuse cases (Trocmé, Fallon, MacLaurin, Daciuk, et al., 2002, Table 4-1(a)).

Figure 3. Forms of abuse and level of injury in cases of substantiated physical abuse (OIS 98)

Abusive inappropriate punishment rather than battered children sustaining severe injuries is far more typical of the types of abuse cases being substantiated by child welfare agencies. By 1998, 71% of substantiated investigations of physical abuse involved inappropriate punishment (Trocmé, Fallon, MacLaurin, Daciuk, et al., 2002, Table 3-5). In fact, nearly one-fifth of all substantiated investigations of child maltreatment involved physical abuse caused by inappropriate punishment.

Sexual abuse decline: Abuser or victim deterrence?

The number of substantiated investigations of sexual abuse decreased by 44%, from 3,400 investigations in 1993 to 1,900 investigations in 1998. This decrease is consistent with decreases reported across the United States (Jones, Finkelhor, & Kopiec, 2001).

Figure 4. Forms of substantiated sexual abuse (OIS 93-98)

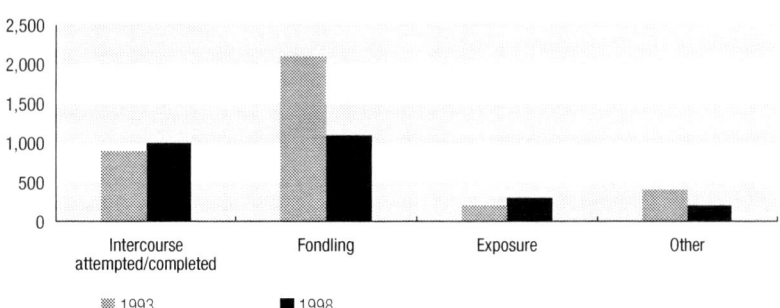

Such a dramatic decrease requires careful analysis. As of yet there is no conclusive evidence to determine whether this decrease can be attributed to a growing reluctance on the part of victims to disclose abuse, hesitancy on the part of parents to report, or to an actual decrease in abuse rates. An actual decrease in abuse rates would be an indication that heightened public awareness, prevention programs, joint police-child welfare investigation protocols, and aggressive charging policies have had a positive effect in deterring abusers.

Alternatively, the decrease could mean that victims and non-offending parents are becoming hesitant to involve authorities. According to this explanation, a criminal court response may be perceived as overly intrusive in some instances and may be deterring victims from reporting. Interestingly, the proportion of substantiated cases involving criminal charges has increased dramatically from 35% in 1993 to 76% in 1998 (Trocmé, McPhee, Kwan Tam, & Hay, 1994, Table 5-4; Trocmé, Fallon, MacLaurin, Daciuk, et al., 2002, Table 5-5).

A full analysis of these changes is currently underway and may help to provide more weight to one of the two explanations. Either way, the policy and practice implications are important. If charging policies and prevention programs have been effective, consideration should be given to expanding these programs to other forms of maltreatment. If, however, criminal charge policies are deterring disclosure, attention will need to be given to developing alternative response protocols. Until there is sufficient evidence to support either strategy, support for research on this question should be a priority.

Neglect and child poverty

The number of substantiated investigations of neglect doubled between 1993 and 1998 from 4,400 investigations to an estimated 8,900 investigations. Increases were noted across all forms of neglect tracked by the OIS 1998, particularly in cases involving inadequate supervision, medical neglect, and permitting maladaptive or criminal behaviour.

While some of this increase may be attributed to growing awareness of the negative effects of child neglect, cuts in social service spending and for services to poor families and the widening income gap between poor and middle class families are also key factors underlying this dramatic increase (see for example Canadian Council on Social Development, 2002). Indeed, of all forms of maltreatment, neglect remains the form of maltreatment the most closely associated with poverty (see for example Drake & Pandey, 1996).

Figure 5. Household characteristics in cases of substantiated neglect compared to other forms of substantiated maltreatment (OIS 98)

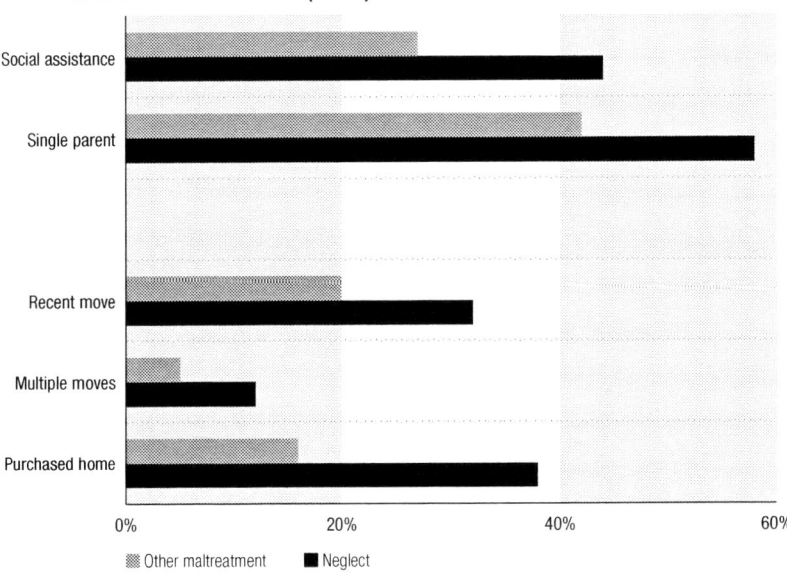

The OIS 1998 found that poverty was most often noted in cases of neglect. Forty-four percent of neglect cases involved families dependent on social assistance, compared to 27% for other forms of maltreatment (Trocmé, Fallon, MacLaurin, Daciuk, et al., 2002, Table 7-5). In contrast, families reported for other forms of maltreatment were much more likely to live in purchased homes (38% vs. 16%) (Trocmé, Fallon, MacLaurin, Daciuk, et al., 2002, Table 7-6 and Table 7-8), and less likely to have moved within the previous six months (20% vs. 32%).

Exposure to domestic violence: Who is the maltreating parent?

The most dramatic increase in the last five years has been with respect to investigations of emotional maltreatment. A nearly nine-fold increase

Community collaboration and differential response

brought the number of substantiated emotional maltreatment investigations from 1,000 investigations in 1993 to 8,700 investigations in 1998.

This increase has been largely driven by investigations involving exposure to domestic violence. Exposure to domestic violence was not separately recorded in the 1993 study. Introduced in the 1998 study as a form of emotional maltreatment, exposure to domestic violence was recorded in nearly 6,000 substantiated investigations, 24% of all substantiated cases (Trocmé, Fallon, MacLaurin, & Copp, 2002, Table 2d).

Since 1993, six provinces have added exposure to domestic violence as a category of maltreatment requiring investigation. Specific reference to exposure to domestic violence was not included in the changes to Ontario's Child and Family Services Act. However, amendments broadening the scope of intervention in cases involving emotional maltreatment may have had some impact on the child welfare response to domestic violence, even though they did not include specific reference to domestic violence.

Figure 6. Forms of substantiated emotional maltreatment (OIS 93-98)

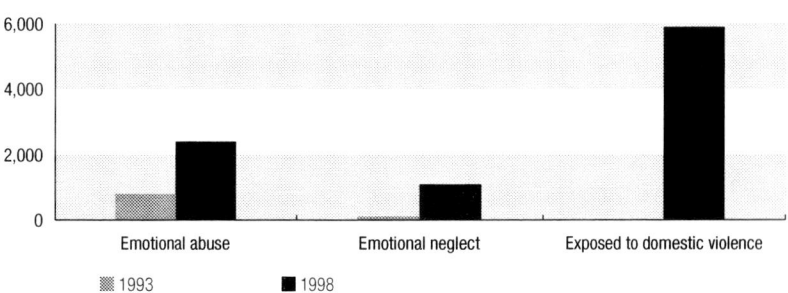

Reports from professionals and in particular, the police, are responsible for most of the increase in exposure to domestic violence cases. This increase requires the development of services and inter-agency protocols designed to meet the needs of these children without further compromising the victimized parent.[2]

The increase in domestic violence cases reflects growing awareness of the effects of exposure to domestic violence on children. The rapid increase in cases is very similar to the increase in sexual abuse cases in the 1980s. Unlike sexual abuse, however, there has not been the same development of services, protocols, and legislation to address the complexities specific to domestic violence cases. In response to the growing number of sexual

---

2 Currently, the Ontario Children's Aid Society Directors of Service network is examining the issue of exposure to domestic violence, its policy implications, and preferred service response.

abuse cases, jurisdictions across Canada developed programs to support victims, protocols to ensure a well-coordinated criminal and child welfare response, and explicit intervention policies designed to remove the perpetrator and keep the victim at home. A similar response is needed to ensure that victims of domestic violence are not put at further risk because they fear losing their children to the child welfare system.

Endangered safety

Along with analyzing the increase in child welfare caseloads by form of maltreatment, it is also important to examine more closely the severity and types of harm investigated by child welfare authorities. Inquiries into the deaths of children under the supervision of child welfare authorities have placed renewed emphasis on the central importance of protecting children from severe harm and, in the most extreme cases, death.

Child homicides

The number of child deaths across Canada classified as homicides has not changed over the past 30 years. The Statistics Canada child homicide survey has documented an average of 86 child homicides per year since 1974. While there is little doubt that a number of child homicides are undetected, there is no reason to think that under-detection is a growing problem. The recent increase in public and media awareness of tragic deaths of maltreated children does not, therefore, reflect an increase in the actual rate of child homicides.

Figure 7. Child homicides in Canada, 1974–2000 (Statistics Canada)

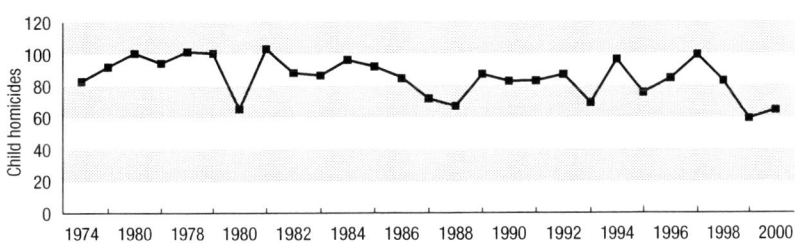

Severe harm

While child deaths are tragic reminders of the potential outcome of severe child abuse and neglect, the protection mandate of child welfare authorities is broader. Severe harm, however, is not a well-defined concept, nor one that is typically tracked by provincial or territorial child welfare information systems. It is particularly important to distinguish between the type of harm that potentially requires urgent intervention (i.e., where failure to intervene immediately could lead to severe harm) versus the type of harm that follows from longer term exposure to chronic maltreatment. The former has shaped much of our current response to suspected child abuse and neglect, with safety-assessments and investigation protocols specifying tight response times and giving child welfare workers authority to intervene rapidly and, if need be, drastically.

A maltreatment-specific estimate of severe harm can be derived from the data collected for 1998 Canadian Incidence Study of Reported Child Abuse and Neglect. Severe physical harm (i.e., broken bones, burns, severe bruises or other injuries severe enough to require medical treatment) was documented in 4% of cases of substantiated abuse or neglect. Neglect of children under three (i.e., children who are young enough that a single incident of neglect could lead to permanent harm) was noted in another 10% of substantiated cases. Sexual abuse, a third type of case in which urgent intervention could be required to protect a child, represents another 10% of substantiated cases. The risk of immediate severe harm is not as well defined, however, in the remaining 76% of substantiated cases of maltreatment.

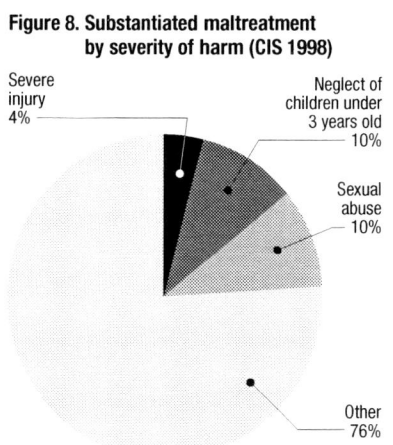

Figure 8. Substantiated maltreatment by severity of harm (CIS 1998)

Re-involving the community*

When the child's development is at risk

The legislation articulating the principles of the various child welfare systems in Canada encompasses terms of reference far broader than child protection alone. An examination of provincial and territorial child welfare laws reveals frameworks that include concepts of children's security, development, and well-being. (See Table 1.)

---

* This section was translated from French by Eve Krakow.

Table 1. Paramount principles in child welfare legislation across Canada

Jurisdiction	Paramount principles for intervention
Alberta	"… survival, security or development of the child is endangered…"
British Columbia	"… the safety and well-being of children are the paramount considerations…"
Manitoba	"The best interests of the child shall be the paramount consideration…"
New Brunswick	"… the security or development of the child is in danger."
Newfoundland	"… every child is entitled to be assured of personal safety, health and well-being…"
Northwest Territories & Nunavut	"… the paramount objective of this Act is to promote the best interests, protection and well-being of children…"
Nova Scotia	"… the paramount consideration in any placement or intervention is best interests of the child."
Ontario	"The paramount purpose of this Act is to promote the best interests, protection and well-being of children."
Prince Edward Island	"… protect children from harm, due to abuse and neglect, within the context of … the best interests of the child."
Quebec	"This Act applies to any child whose security or development is or may be considered to be in danger."
Saskatchewan	"The purpose of this Act is to promote the well-being of children in need of protection…"
Yukon	"… the best interests of the child shall prevail."

In addition to child protection and risk assessment, interventions should aim to prevent the worsening of situations and the intergenerational perpetuation of child maltreatment. This involves meeting children's various needs to enable their healthy and normal growth—both for children in immediate danger and those at risk in the long term.

Child welfare systems, however, have strayed from these objectives to some degree: workers focus primarily on assessing risks rather than meeting needs (Sandau-Beckler, Salcido, Beckler, Mannes, & Beck, 2002). Investigative approaches are dominated by evidence-gathering and verifying that the danger to the child's security has been reduced. Given the inadequate resources granted to child welfare systems by governments, efforts to support families in meeting the needs of children are limited or non-existent.

For example, in Quebec, child welfare interventions are expected to be short term, to reduce state intrusion into families' private lives (Government of Quebec, 1998). Yet in a large proportion of cases, long-term aid is required. The *Quebec Incidence Study of Reported Child Abuse, Neglect, and Serious Behavioural Problems* (*QIS*) found that five main problems were observed in families whose cases were retained by child welfare services in Quebec: poverty, separation or divorce, substance abuse, social isolation, and mental health problems (Tourigny et al., 2002). These families are grappling with multiple difficulties and speed, intensity, and continuity of support are therefore crucial (Macleod, 2000; Salzer & Bickman, 1997). Too often, specialized protection or treatment services are planned in response to a specific single issue, without considering the family as a whole and independent of issues related to maltreatment prevention and child well-being and development. The prevailing paradigm of child welfare services is concerned with danger and focuses on the child's basic needs and security. In this context, interventions directed towards the parents are of a controlling rather than supportive nature (Kamerman & Kahn, 1990; Pelton, 1990).

Yet children need more than protection: they need to be able to develop. Several studies of cases retained by child welfare services in Quebec show that the children experience significant long-term effects on their physical, cognitive, social, emotional, and behavioural development. Their future ability to integrate socially and professionally is often seriously compromised. In addition, the multiple problems experienced by the parents severely limits their ability to support their child's developmental path (Peirson, Laurendeau, & Chamberland, 2001).

Paradigm shift required

Child welfare workers face tremendous challenges and they are often alone in tackling these Herculean responsibilities. This is of particular concern given the alarming increase in the number of cases reported and the considerable internal and external stresses on child welfare systems which seriously hinders workers' ability to provide adequate support to families. These adverse institutional contexts are not yet widely recognized:

> Critics interpret each child's death as the fault of a system that too quickly took the risks to leave children at home and preserve the family. Few took into account that the system is currently under stress with large staff turnover, mounting paperwork, rising costs, declassification of workers, and increasing referrals, often leaving inexperienced workers investigating extremely difficult cases. In addition, the numbers of out-of-home placements is still rising—all in the context of significant funding cuts to social services programs and higher levels of children living in poverty. (Sandau-Beckler et al., 2002, p. 720)

The increased number of child welfare cases across Canada is also indicative of the weakness of the community fabric surrounding these families. Too often, child welfare services are overwhelmed by families with complex, multiple needs. Not only do child welfare service providers feel helpless to manage unwilling (or only slightly willing) families, but they also have a tendency to externalize their responsibilities to the families. It may appear as though child protection systems have withdrawn from the community or were excluded from it. The community not only tends to delegate full responsibility for saving these children to the mandated child welfare institutions, but also to isolate these children from a network of community partners that could in fact be invaluable to them.

Given this void and lack of collaboration, relations between child welfare workers and parents often deteriorate; social control takes over at the expense of social support. For example, the number of cases retained by the Centre jeunesse de Montréal (CJM) but referred to the courts because a service plan agreement cannot be reached with the parents has grown to a rate of 72% in 2001-2002. There has also been a 76% increase since 1997 in the total number of emergency legal appeals involving the CJM (Potvin & Dionne, 2003). More often than not, workers' relationships with families are adversarial and generate mutual mistrust, conflict, and feelings of helplessness (Sandau-Beckler et al., 2002). Under these circumstances, recourse to out-of-home placement is predictable. The number of children in care is in fact on the rise (Lessard, 2002; Kamerman & Kahn, 1990). Placement while the evaluation is being carried out is more probable when the worker notes more than one problem, as well as a greater need of services, for both the parent and the child (Tourigny, Jacob, Poirier, Julien, & Doray, in press). In fact, placement is often considered as a means of coping with the heavy caseload and lack of partners.

A continuum of action

The gap between child welfare systems and the community produces a second cleavage: the objectives of protection and treatment versus those of prevention and promotion. Child welfare has an effective system for handling emergencies, which represent about 25% of the children reported. In light of the increase in reported cases of abuse and neglect and a focus on risk assessment, too little energy is devoted to mitigating the effects of maltreatment on children. Nor is sufficient action taken to deal with exacerbating factors contributing to the recurrence of maltreatment. For example, the duration and recurrence of neglect are especially high. Some studies show that 65% of situations of neglect have been going on for more than six years (Éthier, Couture, & Lacharité, in press; Tourigny et al., 2002). As well, a Quebec study reveals that after 10 years, only 25% of situations of neglect are stopped definitively; 25% are curbed temporarily but then reported again, and 50% require ongoing services (Éthier, Lemelin, & Desaulniers, 2003).

Finally, the children and their families involved with child welfare services are not given sufficient opportunities to grow and flourish. The promotion of well-being is often perceived as a luxury for this clientele and they are frequently denied programs and resources in the community. In this respect, there seems to be confusion between the target and the strategies. Universal programs are organized for the entire population, and targeted programs for groups in certain risk categories, while the prescribed programs are often aimed at groups requiring intensive services (Prillentensky et al., 2001). Promotion and prevention strategies are developed almost exclusively by the organizations that develop universal and selective programs, while treatment and protection are carried out by protection services or second-line organizations providing specialized services. Yet vulnerable families and maltreated children need to be able to access all of the services available in the community. Children need more than security. They also need to be stimulated, to play, and to develop.

In summary, children and families reported to and monitored by child welfare systems have many vulnerabilities and serious problems can affect their prognosis for future development. The community, in its broadest sense, neglects these families; institutions label them and society rejects them. We believe a community-level change is essential to counter this. As noted by Ronnau & Sallee in 1993, among others, child welfare systems and their partners need to be reoriented to better respond to the needs of families, to involve parents in defining intervention plans, and to build on parents' strengths so that they, in turn, can mobilize to support their child's development (cited in Sandau-Beckler et al., 2002; Mallucio, 1990).

An approach centred on needs

An approach centred on children's and families' needs is gaining acceptance in the field (Sandau-Beckler et al., 2002; Hardiker, et al., 2002; Tunnard, 2002; Ward, 1995). In England, the Children Act, introduced in 1989, proved to be a powerful legislative tool that considerably influenced the reorganization of services to children in need, both nationally and locally. This led to the development of standards of practice and performance indicators directed not only towards children's security but also towards their development (Staham & Aldgate, 2003). Studies carried out while this law was being implemented underscored that investigation should not be separated from needs assessment, in the majority of cases.

> The system of separating child protection inquiries and family support assessment was ineffective and counterproductive to meeting the needs of children and families. The studies suggested that, by separating the two systems, some children had missed the

value of early intervention to prevent more intrusive and intensive activity at a later stage. (Statham & Aldgate, 2003, p. 154)

Conversely, Brandon and colleagues (1999) note that allowing security issues to be eclipsed by the more general assessment of needs for services to families also carries the risk of minimizing the danger threatening the child (cited in Statham & Aldgate, 2003). The challenge is therefore to strengthen the links between the assessment of the child's specific needs and the services offered by the various organizations concerned.

In this respect, the tools developed by the Looking After Children project to evaluate needs and monitor children placed in care are very pertinent (Ward & Rose, 2002). Action and assessment records are designed to identify three evaluation components: clear indicators to follow the child's development based on age; the evaluation of the parent's capacities to meet the child's various needs (i.e., basic care, security, stability, love, stimulation, supervision); and family and environmental factors that could affect these parental capacities (i.e., family history and functioning, extended family, social integration, and living conditions). According to some studies, this evaluation grid serves as a valuable reference tool and can be used to establish constructive communication channels between workers and families and to develop intervention plans that are adapted and sensitive to individual children and their families (Statham & Aldgate, 2003). The capacity to develop fruitful partnerships with the family and other organizations is a crucial factor in changing current practices.

Partnerships

Collaboration with the family

Working in partnership with parents is a formidable challenge for social workers. According to Freeman & Hunt (1998) it is not an end in itself but an important means of fostering the child's development, particularly when the intervention is implemented on a voluntary basis (cited in Staham & Aldgate, 2003). The conditions contributing to the successful creation of a collaborative relationship must be present at all stages of the evaluation process, specifically referral, assessment, planning, implementation of the intervention plan (Sandau-Beckler et al., 2002; Brun & Rapp, 2001; Staham & Aldgate, 2003).

Building a partnership with the child is equally necessary. The Children Act is particularly innovative on this point, insisting on the importance of allowing children to express their desires and feelings as well as ensuring the child is included in the planning and decision-making process.

Collaboration with the community

If child welfare workers are to better respond to the various needs of the families they serve, they need to be able to rely on community resources, such as family resource centres that welcome all families and offer a range of services and activities. Additional strategies include developing partnerships with other family-serving agencies and neighbourhood community organizations. Ensuring proper coordination among various services is a priority. The Children Act details the basic principles of a working relationship among different organizations representing a range of sectors, including health, social services, education, and housing. However, studies by Statham (2001) on the implementation of this legislation show that assessment, planning, implementation, and follow-up of the intervention plans were very slow to be developed (cited in Statham & Aldgate, 2003).

The fragmentation of mandates and budgets is a serious obstacle to mobilizing all stakeholders to consider the whole child. However, there are some encouraging examples of collaborative practices between child protection services and community organizations (Aldgate & Bradley, 1999). More explicit measures must be taken to stimulate collaborative working toward common objectives and activities. There needs to be a greater sharing of resources, which sometimes means merging budgets. Finally, coordination mechanisms must be clear so that agreements are established on solid and durable foundations.

In summary, interventions must be more holistic, intersectoral, and go beyond individual interests. The fragmentation of aid, resulting from the strict definitions of organizational mandates, affects the allocation of human resources, compartmentalizes the work, and results in parallelism, redundancy, and sometimes competition between organizations (White, Jobin, McCann, & Morin, 2002). These issues must be resolved in the child and family's interest as they have a right to receive the best support possible. Figure 9 illustrates the desired relationships to be developed across community sectors.

Figure 9. Shared and convergent objectives among the services available within the community

Specialized services (to protect children and reduce negative effects)	Child and his/her family	**Other community services** (to ensure the child's overall development and to improve the living conditions and lifestyle habits of the families)
• Preventive services • Child protection • Legal system • Police • Hospitals		• Church, mosque, synagogue • School • Daycare • Employment/housing • Recreation/sports • Community centres

Levels of action

The entire community must be called upon to assist vulnerable children and their families, at all levels. For example, integrating a child into a therapy group for sexually abused children can help in expressing feelings and reduce isolation. Integrating a parent into a professional development program can help alleviate depression, increase income, offer access to a more diversified social network, and provide a positive example to the children. In other words, preventive activities can promote the development of the children and the parents.

If we are to modify the life trajectories of maltreated children, we must develop three broad lines of action. First are those focusing on child protection and treatment, implemented by child protection services. Secondly are actions linked to prevention and the promotion of well-being, which decrease the risk factors, increase resilience, and provide opportunities for children, youth, and parents; these programs are universal or targeted. The third level of action, too often neglected by workers in psychosocial intervention sectors, concerns improving living conditions. This is generally the responsibility of housing, transportation, employment, or economic development sectors. The precarious living conditions of families involved with child welfare services no longer need to be proven, especially in cases of neglect (Tourigny et al., 2002; Trocmé et al., 2001). Parental competencies are, of course, a necessary condition for taking care of and educating a child; however, they are not sufficient in themselves. These families live in dire situations that need to be improved. A synthesis of potential actions is presented in Table 2.

Table 2. Possible levels of action

Targets	Examples
Access to specialized clinical services	• Group therapy for sexually abused children • Support groups for children in foster care • Counselling for adult substance abusers • Shelter for battered women • Individual therapy
Development and consolidation of programs for parents and their children	• Homework assistance • Early reading program • Recreation, music, sports programs • Parenting classes • Day camps • Respite care • Educational field trips • Conflict resolution program
Improvement of families' living conditions and lifestyle habits	• Access to clean and safe housing • Employability program • Transportation service • Group kitchens

Conclusion

Child maltreatment is a multidimensional social problem. The severity and types of maltreatment call for more detailed analyses. More extreme forms of maltreatment may require a rigorous and cautious investigation of the dangers whereas less serious forms may require a holistic child and family-centred needs approach. Children and families reported to child protection services are a heterogeneous clientele and require diverse responses, ranging from short-term, crisis intervention with a family preservation approach to long-term, continuous support. Child protection systems must be able to vary their strategies and effectively collaborate with the legal system, specialized treatment services, and community programs. But whatever the objectives of the intervention plan, child welfare workers can no longer work alone.

Evaluating the implementation of assessment tools in the Australian child protection system

Jim Barber and Della Knoke

Abstract

Actuarial instruments are being widely implemented within child welfare to inform and guide decisions about whether and/or what form of services are most appropriate for children and families. The promise of improved decision making with the use of actuarial instruments derives from their empirical foundations and demonstration of adequate validity and reliability. However, the extent to which these psychometric properties are preserved in the field depends on how these instruments are implemented. This chapter describes the introduction in two Australian states of tiered responding based upon actuarial assessment instruments. In the state of South Australia, some degree of training was provided prior to implementation of new processes and instruments. However, no pilot testing was performed on the instruments and no provision was made for modifications to the system in the field. An internal case audit recently suggested that the system is not operating as its proponents had hoped. In contrast, the introduction of actuarial safety and risk assessment instruments in Queensland was accompanied by some effort to monitor implementation of the new system and its effectiveness. The identification of difficulties facilitated the development of strategies to improve validity and reliability of case prioritization.

Introduction

In Australia, actuarial risk and safety assessment is rapidly replacing professional judgment in the task of deciding whether or not to respond to child protection notifications (reports of maltreatment). The adoption of actuarial approaches reflects an increased acceptance of evidence based practice (Camasso & Jagannathan, 2000) and dissatisfaction with unreliability of clinical judgment in assessing risk of future maltreatment (Baird & Wagner, 2000; Rossi, Schuerman, & Budde, 1996). The promise of actuarial assessment tools lies in their potential to improve the consistency (reliability) and validity of decision making.

Actuarial models are based on the empirical study of child protection cases and their future maltreatment outcomes. Validity is established through the identification of factors that are statistically related to the occurrence of future maltreatment. Identified factors are utilized to construct a questionnaire that can be scored in a mechanical fashion that is consistent across cases and settings. Since actuarial instruments yield a quantitative assessment of risk, they lend themselves readily to prioritization of notifications: high scores need an urgent response, low scores do not. Within differential response frameworks, where there is more than one system response option, the task becomes determining which forms of service are most appropriate for each case. Assignment to the appropriate service stream or track is predicated on the assumption that cases requiring different forms of service can be accurately differentiated in the assessment/intake process.

Implementation fidelity

Establishing adequate reliability and validity in a research context is obviously essential before any new decision making tool can be introduced. However, the extent to which these psychometric properties are preserved when instruments are implemented in the field depends upon how these tools are implemented. The inappropriate or inconsistent application of assessment criteria may compromise both the reliability and validity of instruments.

Implementation fidelity refers to how well a program or intervention has been put into practice. The implementation fidelity construct recognizes that fidelity exists on a continuum and that interventions, typically developed in more controlled settings, will be adapted to the practice settings and situations in which they are applied. Research indicates that: a) variability within and across practice settings may compromise implementation fidelity and b) how well an intervention has been implemented influences outcomes (Durlak, 1998). Inadequate implementation, referred to as a Type III error, compromises evaluation of outcomes by making it difficult to discern whether outcomes are related to the intervention as designed or to variations in implementation. Focusing on outcome evaluation, without also evaluating the implementation process, may lead to erroneous conclusions (Basch, Sliepcevich, Gold, Duncan, & Kolbe, 1985).

Within the context of decision making in child welfare, adequate implementation fidelity requires that the use of actuarial assessment tools in the field corresponds to their intended use. Problems with implementation of risk models have been noted in child welfare (Doueck, Levine, & Bronson,1990; Martinez, 1987). Inconsistent application of assessment criteria may lead to discrepant priority ratings for the same or similar cases. Despite the impact that such consistencies may have on the services delivered and outcomes for children and families, how well risk assessment processes are implemented has rarely been examined.

This chapter examines the implementation of actuarial assessment tools in the Australian child welfare system. First, the case of South Australia will be examined. A variety of implementation problems were revealed in a recent audit in South Australia, a state that provided little training and no pilot testing of the instruments adopted in practice. In contrast, in Queensland, the process of implementing a new actuarial assessment instrument was accompanied by a process to assess and improve the reliability and validity of the instrument in the field. Three studies conducted during this process in Queensland will be reviewed, each underscoring the value of quality control measures in the course of implementation.

South Australia

The importance of assessing the reliability and validity of assessment instruments in the field is exemplified by recent experiences in South Australia. The implementation of actuarial risk assessment resulted from recommendations of a Ministry Child Protection Task Force (Hetherington, 1999), which found, inter alia, that responses to notifications were inconsistent and driven to a considerable extent by resource constraints. Improvements in consistency in response and decision making were sought through the use of empirically-based assessment tools that were brief and user friendly. Among the stated objectives of the new assessment process were "target[ing] investigative resources to children in immediate danger and at significant risk and provide less intrusive and non-investigative responses to low risk reports" and "target[ing] departmental intervention where abuse has been confirmed and to those cases where children are at high risk of re-abuse."

In its reform of child protective services, South Australia introduced tiered responding and new actuarial instruments to assess initial safety, immediate safety and, among cases of confirmed abuse, family strengths, and needs. The initial safety assessment tool, originally designed by the New York Department and Albany University in the 1980s, consisted of 12 case characteristics that, taken together, constitute a set of potentially abusive or threatening acts perpetrated by an adult against a child. Identification of any item indicates that the child may be in imminent danger and therefore, a Tier 1 (immediate danger of serious maltreatment) or Tier 2 (immediate or significant risk of maltreatment) classification is warranted. A second safety assessment is undertaken using the same instrument for all Tier 1 and 2 classifications. If the initial assessment results are confirmed, a separate assessment of immediate safety is conducted, yielding four possible risk levels—very high, high, moderate and low—depending upon the score attained. Although the instrument produces a score, workers are permitted to override ratings derived from the instrument on the basis of their professional judgment, provided that the decision to do so is briefly explained. In addition, cases of confirmed abuse are subjected to a structured needs and strengths assessment, designed by the Wisconsin Children's Research Center. If the family is judged to be high on both risk and need, the worker proceeds to a guided decision making protocol which is intended to result in a comprehensive case plan. If either risk or need is not high, however, the worker is directed to take minimal corrective action (such as referral to another agency) and to end intervention at that point. Tier 3 classification is reserved for cases where there may be a high level of need but the risk of maltreatment is low, at least in the short term. Cases with a Tier 3 notification are invited to attend a meeting to examine options for addressing the concerns raised by the notification.

Some degree of training was provided prior to implementation but no pilot testing was performed on the instruments in their new context and no provision was made for modifications to the system in the field. Problems with implementation of the instruments were apparent in a recent internal document reporting the results of 70 case audits of Tier 1 and Tier 2 notifications, obtained by the author under freedom of information legislation. In their report, the auditors (two senior practitioners), concluded that:

> Overall, the consistent picture that emerges from the … audit … is one of widespread non-compliance or under compliance with service standards. The pattern is one which more clearly reflects outright omission of required processes than it does actual attempts to adhere which somehow go awry (e.g., through poor judgment, or faulty reasoning). This suggests either ignorance of practice requirements or systematic corner-cutting in response to overload, or both. (South Australia Department of Human Services, 2002, pp. 5–6)

In addition, the report indicated that second stage safety assessments were either poorly conducted or not at all, there was a low degree of congruence between risk and needs assessments and there was "wholesale underachievement of service level requirements" (p. 6) in high risk–high needs cases.

Despite the development and implementation of an assessment process designed to improve the accuracy of risk assessment, the instruments were not implemented in a way that could satisfy this objective. The case of South Australia clearly illustrates that the introduction of actuarial instruments into practice does not necessarily ensure valid or reliable classification of cases nor adherence to a standardized assessment protocol.

Queensland

Queensland is the latest Australian state to base its priority ratings upon actuarial risk assessment. Prior to revising its child protection system, Queensland child protection workers were already accustomed to assigning notifications to a Priority 1, 2, or 3 level of urgency (corresponding to the criteria for Tier 1, 2, and 3 classification, respectively). However, professional judgment provided the basis for these judgments. Under the revised system, more objective bases for classifications at intake have gradually been implemented within three pilot regions: Central Queensland (regional), Toowoomba (metropolitan), and the Gold Coast (metropolitan). Separate intake and investigation teams were formed within each of these regions, with intake workers trained to conduct stage 1 safety assessments before handing cases over for further investigation. At the intake stage, workers have two fundamental responsibilities: (a) to assign a priority rating to incoming notifications and (b) to arrange with the investigating District centre office the response relevant to their rating.

The remainder of this paper describes the quality control measures developed in Queensland and applied in three regions that have implemented the new intake Risk, Harm, and Safety Assessment protocol.

Validity and reliability

A crucial measure of system effectiveness is the validity of the judgment made regarding case prioritization. In the studies below, validity refers to the extent to which the priority rating at intake reflects the likelihood of future maltreatment. Validity was assessed three ways. First, false negatives were operationally defined as a case designated as a Priority 3 classification that was both re-notified and substantiated within three months of the initial judgment. Increases in the rate of false negatives with the implementation of the new intake instrument would suggest that children at high risk were being misclassified as low risk and thus were less likely to receive protective responses under the new system.

Second, false positives were defined as Priority 1 cases that were not substantiated at the investigation stage. Increases in the rate of false positives would suggest that the new system had become more conservative, resulting in more cases being investigated unnecessarily.

As a third index of validity, four senior (expert) practitioners from the department constructed a number of hypothetical cases to which they assigned priority rankings, according to the process described below in Study 1. Next, trainee intake workers independently assigned a priority rating to each of these hypothetical cases and levels of agreement between the trainees and the experts were calculated. Thus, expert ratings were used as the criterion or yardstick with which to gauge how well worker ratings corresponded to the "correct" rating for each case.

In addition to these measures of validity, inter-rater reliability was also evaluated in Study 1 and Study 2. Inter-rater reliability assesses the extent to which assessments produce consistent results across workers.

Study 1

The first study involved assessments of reliability and validity during training sessions in which intake workers were introduced and trained to use the instrument for prioritizing notifications and referring Priority 1 and 2 cases for investigation. Four case scenarios were constructed by a training team of four senior practitioners, responsible for implementing the new protocol. Following thorough discussion and consensus, the training team assigned each case a priority ranking. According to the team, Cases 1 and 2 warranted a Priority 2 rating, while Cases 3 and 4 required a Priority 1 rating.

To examine consistency in priority ratings, the level of agreement among workers was examined before and after training on the new instrument. In addition, the level of agreement on priority ratings between intake workers and the training team was examined as previously indicated.

Sixty-six intake workers from the three pilot regions of Gold Coast, Central Queensland, and Toowoomba were included in the trial. Forty-four of the respondents were from the Gold Coast and assigned to three different training groups based on their local office. Six intake workers from Toowoomba and 16 from central Queensland were assigned to the fourth and fifth training groups, respectively.

Procedure

The training team allocated Cases 1 and 4 to the pre-training portion of the trial. During this phase, all participants were required to assign to each case a priority rating using the professional judgment they were accustomed to employing in the field. Respondents were instructed not to confer but to arrive at their judgments independently of each other. Following training in the use of the new assessment protocol, respondents were asked to prioritize Cases 2 and 3 using the new Risk, Harm, and Safety Assessment instrument.

Results

Table 1 presents the level of agreement of ratings within groups and the priority ratings that each training group assigned to the four case scenarios, adjusted for chance. Twenty ratings were provided, with 10 pre- and 10 post-training (2 cases × 5 groups at each time). The level of agreement reflects the extent to which the same cases receive similar priority ratings across workers. The pre-training level of agreement varied across groups, ranging from a low of 0.50 to a high of 1.00 (perfect agreement). Judged against the conventional reliability benchmark of 0.70 or better (Nunnally, 1967), one half of the pre-training groups failed to reach this criterion using professional judgment. Post training results indicate that all but one group met this criterion using the actuarial instrument.

Table 1. Training group responses to four case scenarios and levels of agreement (adjusted for chance) before and after training

Regional Office	n	Pre-training		Post-training	
		Case 1	Case 4	Case 2	Case 3
Gold Coast Grp. 1	13				
Priority 1		9		10	
Priority 2		4	13	3	13
Priority 3					
Agreement		0.69	1.00	0.77	1.00
Toowoomba & Sth. West	6				
Priority 1			1	1	5
Priority 2		6	5	5	1
Priority 3					
Agreement		1.00	0.83	0.83	0.83
Gold Coast Grp. 2	22				
Priority 1		3	7	6	19
Priority 2		19	14	16	2
Priority 3					
Agreement		0.86	0.67	0.73	0.91
Central Qld.	16				
Priority 1		5	9	9	15
Priority 2		11	6	6	
Priority 3					
Agreement		0.67	0.59	0.59	1.00
Gold Coast Grp. 3	9				
Priority 1		2	4	8	8
Priority 2		7	5		
Priority 3					
Agreement		0.78	0.50	1.00	1.00

Note: Some responses to some case scenarios were missing.

When differences in training group ratings for each case were examined statistically using analyses of variance (ANOVA) and post-hoc tests (LSD), the level of disagreement was statistically significant in 2 of the 4 cases. Specifically, analyses of Case 1 (pre-training) and Case 2 (post-training) showed significant disagreement in priority ratings across groups of workers ($p<.01$ and $p<.001$, respectively). Thus, even though the level of agreement after training was more likely to meet the criterion of 0.70, significant inconsistency in priority ratings was noted among workers whether judgments were based upon either professional judgment or the actuarial assessment tool.

As illustrated in Table 2, differences in the level of agreement between workers and experts were also evident across training groups (regions), with a low of 0.00 to a high of 1.00 (perfect agreement). Each regional office showed poor agreement on at least one case. When the ratings of all intake workers were combined and compared with ratings of the training team ("experts"), the level of agreement ranged from a 0.24 (Case 4) to 0.95 (Case 3). With the exception of Case 3, there was little consistency between the ratings assigned by trainees and the correct ratings assigned to cases by experts.

Table 2. Training group levels of agreement (adjusted for chance) with correct responses broken down by Regional Office

Regional Office	n	Pre-training		Post-training	
		Case 1	Case 4	Case 2	Case 3
Gold Coast Grp. 1	13	0.30	0.00	0.06	1.00
Toowoomba & Sth. West	6	1.00	0.00	0.83	0.83
Gold Coast Grp. 2	22	0.86	0.16	0.73	0.86
Central Qld.	16	0.69	0.55	0.27	1.00
Gold Coast Grp. 3	9	0.78	0.30	0.00	1.00
Total	66	0.71	0.24	0.46	0.95
Correct Response		Priority 2	Priority 1	Priority 2	Priority 1

Discussion

In summary, Study 1 found that regional offices not only differed from the training team in their ratings but also from each other. Neither professional judgment nor the new Risk, Harm, and Safety Assessment could be considered reliable at the time the implementation trial commenced. The fact that training groups in Study 1 differed among themselves suggests that systematic differences between regions existed in their handling of child protection notifications. It follows that a child would likely receive a different priority rating depending upon which regional office was approached. A possible explanation for this phenomenon is that regional office priority thresholds are influenced by the level of demand for their services: the greater the demand, the higher the threshold for entry to Priority 1.

By way of mitigation, almost all of the differences observed in Study 1 were one rather then two points in magnitude. In other words, in almost every case, discrepancies in ratings were between Priority 1 and Priority 2, rather than a much more serious disagreement between assigned ratings of Priority 1 and Priority 3.

Poor validity of worker judgments was evident in the discrepancy between worker and expert priority ratings. Whether professional judgment or the actuarial instrument was employed to prioritize cases, the criteria being used to assign ratings were not successful in producing ratings that reflected their "true" priority level, as represented by expert judgments.

Despite these somewhat equivocal results, the Queensland Department of Families proceeded to implement the new intake assessment in the pilot regions but made a commitment to follow up training trials in an effort to improve the reliability and validity of the assessment instrument. The experts raters who participated in the trial also undertook to perform periodic checks and debriefing within the field in an effort to promote greater consistency as the trial proceeded. As described below in Study 2, reliability and validity of worker ratings were assessed again after this additional in-field training.

Study 2

Study 2 occurred six months after the system had been implemented and assessed the impact of training in the field (monitoring and debriefing) on reliability and validity of the Risk, Harm, and Safety Assessment. Prior to a follow-up training session, intended to re-assess and, if necessary, re-train intake workers in their use of the stage 1 safety assessment instrument, intake workers were asked to assign priority ratings to three new hypothetical cases. Since the system was operational by this time, it was not possible to take all 65 workers off line at one time for follow-up training.

Methods

Thirteen intake workers were chosen at random from the three pilot regions. Four workers were drawn from the Gold Coast Regional Office, five from Toowoomba and South West and four from Central Queensland. Three prioritized case scenarios were constructed by the training team following the procedure referred to in Study 1. According to the training team experts, two of the cases were Priority 1 and one case was a Priority 2. The three case scenarios were presented to respondents at the start of the training session. Respondents were given no coaching or debriefing prior to making their ratings.

Results

The results, presented in Table 3, indicated that this time there were very high levels of agreement within and between regional offices on all three cases. In addition, the levels of agreement between workers and experts were near perfect for all cases. Thus, the data suggest that priority ratings were both reliable (consistent) and valid (correct responses) following additional in-field monitoring and training.

Table 3. Responses to the three case scenarios in follow-up trials

	n	Case 1	Case 2	Case 3
Gold Coast Grp. 1	4			
Priority 1			4	1
Priority 2		4		
Priority 3				
Agreement		1.00	1.00	1.00
Toowoomba & Sth.West	5			
Priority 1			5	5
Priority 2		5		
Priority 3				
Agreement		1.00	1.00	1.00
Central Qld.	4			
Priority 1		1	4	4
Priority 2		3		
Priority 3				
Agreement		0.72	1.00	1.00
TOTAL	13			
Priority 1		1	13	13
Priority 2		12		
Priority 3				
Agreement		.092	1.00	1.00

Discussion

While these results are encouraging, an obvious limitation of the study is the very small sample size involved in the exercise. For this reason the Queensland Department of Families plans to work systematically through all of the remaining pilot workers over the coming months until reliability and validity data are acceptable for all intake workers. Once the trial results are satisfactory, the new intake system will gradually be extended to each regional office using the methods described in Studies 1 and 2.

Study 3

To assess the effect of the implementation trial in the field (November 2001 to April 2002), two types of comparison were made using secondary data obtained from Queensland's central administrative database. The central database contains case-level information on notifications, prioritization and investigation outcome. Using these data, priority ratings, expressed as a percentage of total notifications during the six months following implementation, were compared with data collected in precisely the same months in the previous year, in an effort to control for seasonal variations (within-region comparisons). Post-implementation data on false positives and false negatives were also compared across pilot regions and/or with "other Queensland," meaning those regions within Queensland that did not implement the new system.

Results

Figure 1 illustrates the dramatic increase in priority ratings that accompanied the introduction of the new system. The percentage of Priority 1 ratings increased substantially in all three pilot regions, coupled with a decline in the percentage of Priority 3 notifications. These increases are in direct contrast to the rest of Queensland where there was little change in priority ratings over time. One possible explanation for the increase in priority ratings following implementation of the new system is that intake workers erred on the side of caution and assigned to notifications a higher level of urgency than was warranted. To examine this possibility the rate of false positives is examined next.

Figure 1. Percentage change in child protection notifications from Nov '00–Apr '01 to Nov '01–Apr '02 comparing PR1, PR2, and PR3 notifications

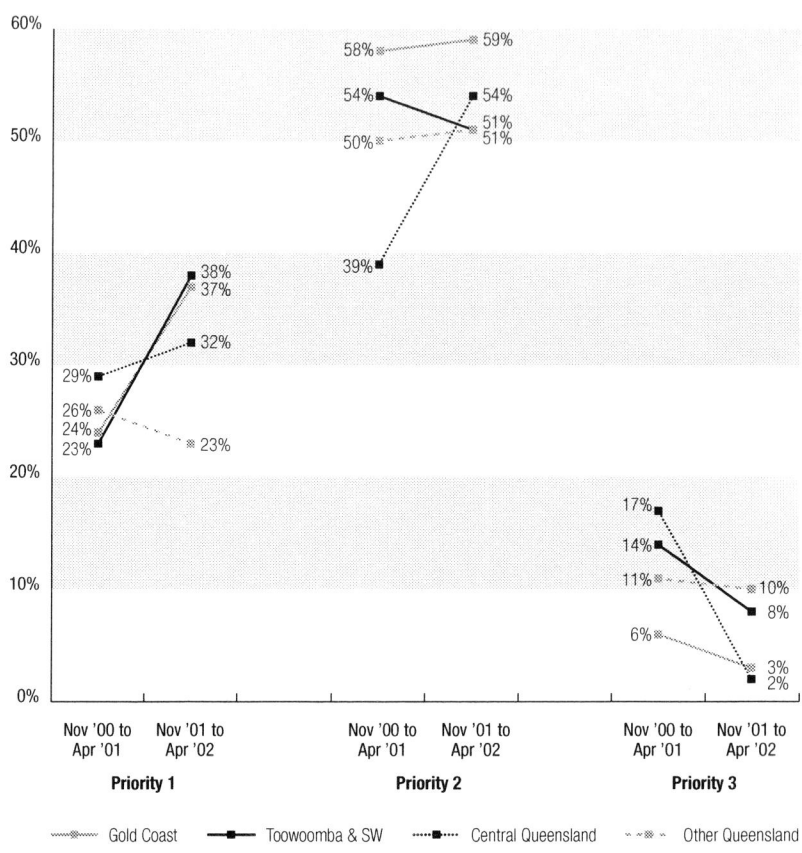

Source: Department of Families, WAP Data (Alternate data source to Statistical Services).

To compare the rates of false positives pre- and post-implementation, the Gold Coast pilot region was compared with regions of Queensland not involved in the trial. (The two other pilot regions, Toowoomba and Central Queensland, had such small numbers of Priority 1 cases that they had to be excluded from this analysis.) As previously indicated, false positives were operationally defined as the percentage of Priority 1 cases that were unsubstantiated at the investigation stage. Figure 2 illustrates that, whereas the rate of false positive notifications remained relatively stable across the rest of the state, the immediate effect of the new actuarial safety instrument was to produce a short-term increase in false positives within the pilot region. This transitory increase was apparent relative to other Queensland and relative to the within-region pattern evident in the months prior to implementation.

Figure 2. Number of Priority 1 cases that were unsubstantiated comparing four months of pre-Regional Intake Team data with Regional Intake Team trial data*

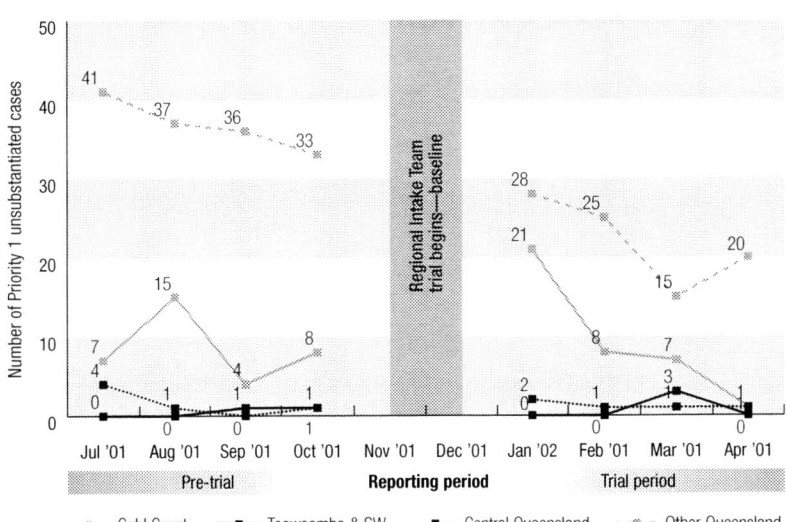

*Due to data collection issues, data for November and December 2001 were excluded from analysis.
Source: Department of Families, Statistical Services Branch, as at June 20, 2002.

As previously indicated, false negatives were operationally defined as Priority 3 cases that were considered at intake to not require investigation but which re-emerged as re-notifications that were substantiated within three months. The rate of false negatives was examined to consider the possibility that workers had become less accurate in identifying Priority 3 cases. However, the number of false negatives was negligible across pilot regions and in comparison regions (other Queensland), ranging from a low of 0 to a high of 8 cases over the course of post-implementation follow up. Thus, the only safe interpretation of the data is that false negatives as defined are a very rare occurrence throughout Queensland.

Discussion

Secondary analysis of data extracted from the Queensland Department of Families dataset suggested that the short-term consequences of introducing the new actuarial approach and separating intake and investigative functions included an increase in the number of cases assigned a Priority 1 rating and a short-term increase in the rate of false positives. As the trial proceeded, this phenomenon abated. The decline in the rate of false positives in the months following implementation corresponded to the period in which in-field training was implemented, suggesting that with additional training, the rate of case misclassification was reduced. However, it is impossible to determine whether the increased conservatism that accompanied Queensland's new system was attributable to the new instrument, to the separation of assessment and investigation, or both since these innovations were introduced simultaneously. It is possible that when workers are relieved of the responsibility for conducting an investigation, they are more inclined to take a conservative approach to the need for investigation.

Other implementation issues

Though the present chapter has focused on assessing validity and reliability of actuarial instruments in the field, the new approach to intake assessment adopted by Queensland also introduced new investigation timelines. According to departmental regulations, Priority 1 investigations must begin within 24 hours and Priority 2 investigations within 14 days of notification. Examination of the central database revealed large variation in Priority 1 response times across pilot regions; in fact, 24-hour response times could not be guaranteed in any part of Queensland. Similarly, responding to Priority 2 investigations on time was the exception rather than the rule. These findings suggest that each component of new initiatives needs to be carefully monitored to establish the level of adherence to new protocols.

Discussion and conclusions

Taken together the results of the three studies described above illustrate several important points about the conduct of risk assessment in the field. First, case prioritization based on professional judgment was found to be unreliable in Queensland's pilot regions. Second, immediately following training in the use of an actuarial approach, the reliability and validity of the new approach remained equivocal. However, following implementation in the field supported by periodic checks and discussion of sample case files led by the experts responsible for system change, the measurement properties of the new instrument improved. That is, the data suggest that the opportunity to debrief and discuss cases in the field improved consistency and increased the extent to which worker ratings corresponded to expert ratings.

In view of the small number of cases and workers involved in the studies described, it is impossible to extrapolate much beyond the individuals involved in the studies. In addition, the exclusion of two pilot regions (Study 3) due to the small number of false positives, limited the analysis of post-implementation misclassifications to only one pilot region. These limitations are illustrative of the compromises that are often required when an evidence based approach is taken to system change (Barber & Dunstone, in press). Although we cannot always achieve methodological perfection in the field, we can adopt methodologically sound principles and apply them as best we can according to whatever constraints happen to prevail in the field at the time.

Despite the limitations in the studies described, they do underscore that an adequate level of implementation fidelity needs to be established, not simply assumed. Both South Australia and Queensland incorporated some training in the use of actuarial decision making tools prior to implementation. However, pilot testing and/or post-implementation evaluation revealed that the assessment processes and instruments were not implemented entirely as intended. Within the context of assessment for service allocation or case tracking, establishing an adequate pre-implementation level of reliability and validity in worker judgments would minimize both over- and under-inclusion of cases in the investigative response stream.

While it is possible to examine implementation fidelity after the fact, retrospective caseworker interviews and file reviews may yield inaccurate or incomplete information regarding specific processes (Doueck, et al., 1992). Pilot testing such as occurred in Queensland is clearly preferable. In addition, qualitative and quantitative data, collected during the implementation process, will cast light on any aspects of the protocol that are not adequately implemented and why (Basch et al., 1985).

Alternative response to child protective services investigations in the United States

Diana English, John D. Fluke, and Ying-Ying T. Yuan

Abstract

In the United States, numerous states have implemented alternative responses to child protective services (CPS). The present chapter examines two aspects of these initiatives. First, the findings of a two-year National Study of CPS and Reform Efforts revealed the scope and characteristics of alternative response services (ARS) implemented across the United States. ARS are being practised more than expected and nearly one-half of the states reported having alternative response policies. Implementation of ARS varied across agencies surveyed. However, in general, ARS initiatives sought to provide less intrusive services and to facilitate access to and engagement in services for families with lower risk or lower severity of maltreatment, without labeling caretakers as perpetrators. Second, an evaluation of the ARS model implemented in Washington State underscores the importance of assessing outcomes of these new initiatives and the assumptions underlying ARS models.

This study revealed that a minority of the ARS families actually engaged in (i.e., used) services. The rate of re-referral among families receiving ARS was comparable to families not served or families receiving CPS services as usual. In addition, many more families were identified as needing service than received services. Though ARS presents the potential for a broader more flexible set of responses to child welfare referrals, the processes and objectives of alternative models must be clearly articulated and evaluated.

Introduction

During the past several years there have been increased calls to rethink child protective services. Concerns about child protective services (CPS) include role conflicts related to the investigation versus service functions, and questions about whether CPS is too intrusive, or not intrusive enough. The CPS system in the United States is charged with identifying and preventing further maltreatment of children. It is operated by a mixture of state and local authorities based on the needs and conditions of these jurisdictions under a broad federal mandate. Recently, the development of response approaches that present alternatives to CPS investigations has emerged as a means to address real or perceived limitations associated with traditional investigations. Among the purposes of alternative responses are the provision of a less intrusive response to address less serious maltreatment, to avoid labeling caregivers as perpetrators, to facilitate access to necessary services for families who may be at risk of subsequent maltreatment, and to encourage the engagement of families so that they will take advantage of services.

A number of states have been moving toward the development of an alternative response to CPS. Several models of alternative response services (ARS) have been developed. One ARS model separates CPS functions into two tracks. In one track, the primary CPS role is assessment. In the assessment track, the primary role of the CPS worker is to assess families' needs and refer to community-based programs for service. In the other track, investigation remains the primary focus, often with joint police and social worker investigations. In these ARS models, the majority of referrals (e.g., two-thirds) may be assigned to assessment. A second ARS model is to divert less serious CPS referrals that meet specific criteria to community-based programs for assessment and service. Despite similarities in principles and objectives, there is variation across the United States as to how ARS models are implemented in practice.

There are several assumptions underlying this move to rethink CPS. For example, there is an assumption that information at CPS intake is sufficient to adequately identify families appropriate for diversion to less intrusive services. There is also an assumption that families will voluntarily engage in services, there are available resources to meet service needs, and that social workers have the skills necessary to engage families and know which families to target for voluntary services.

Evaluations of early ARS programs raise some fundamental questions about the underlying theory and assumptions about what these programs can accomplish. Early outcome data from several state ARS programs (primarily CPS investigation and assessment type models) indicated that between 12% and 36% of families investigated by CPS actually engaged in services (Schene, 2001). The evaluation revealed that engagement rates were comparable in assessment and investigation tracks. Many more families were assessed as needing services than actually engaged in services. Only one of the three evaluations examined re-referral rates—about 25% of the investigated cases were re-referred and 16% of the alternative response cases were re-referred. Thus, future evaluations of ARS will need to determine the extent to which objectives are being achieved by current practices.

This chapter summarizes key results of two recent studies related to alternative response in the United States. These studies have different but complementary foci. The first, is a national overview of CPS, the National Study of Child Protective Services and Reform Efforts, sponsored by the Administration on Children, Youth and Families, Administration for Children and Families, and the Office of the Assistant Secretary for Planning and Evaluation of the US Department of Health and Human Services. This study examines how alternative response models are conceptualized and implemented across agencies that provide alternatives to CPS throughout the United States. The second study is an evaluation of a specific diversified response approach in Washington State and was conducted by the Office of Children's Administration Research of the Children's Administration, Department of Social and Health Services.

National Study of CPS Systems and Reform Efforts

Purpose and methods

The objective of the two-year National Study of Child Protective Services Systems and Reform Efforts was to report on the current status of child protective services in the United States to provide a snapshot of the system as of 2001.[1] The study focused on the functional areas of CPS intake, investigation, and alternative response. Special attention was given to newly emerging practices to improve services to abused and neglected children and their families. In addition to a literature review, the study conducted an analysis of written CPS policy in all states and the District of Columbia, a survey of the practices of 300 randomly selected local CPS agencies, and site visits to some of the agencies that had reported innovative practices in the local agency survey. The study addressed findings and new directions, including those identified at a symposium of persons knowledgeable of

---

1 The National Study of Child Protective Services and Systems Reform Efforts was conducted by Walter R. McDonald & Associates, Inc. (WRMA), with the assistance of the American Humane Association, KRA Corporation, and Westat, Inc., under contract number HHS-100-00-0017. The authors are pleased to acknowledge Laura Radel of the Office of the Assistant Secretary for Planning and Evaluation at HHS and Catherine Nolan, the Director of Office of Child Abuse and Neglect of the Children's Bureau at HHS for their assistance in the preparation of this document and who jointly managed the study on behalf of HHS. We would also like to acknowledge the efforts of our colleagues on the project team.

CPS policies and practices that was held as a part of the study process.[2]

Policy summaries were derived from both written materials and interviews. The most recent state policy manuals as of 2001 were examined for all 50 states and the District of Columbia. A topical outline was developed that focused on administrative structure, screening and intake, investigation, and alternative response. Items of interest were identified for each broad category, and information in these areas was verified through phone interviews with knowledgeable CPS personnel in each state.

The second study component consisted of a survey that examined the functions and operational practices of local agencies needed to meet the state and local mandates and policy requirements. This component was addressed through a local agency survey (LAS) of a nationally representative sample of 375 local CPS agencies and, of these, 300 (80%) responded to the survey. The survey consisted of five modules: Administration, Screening/Intake, Investigation Response, Other CPS Response (alternative response), and New Directions. For each module, the person most knowledgeable about CPS practice in the particular topical or functional area was asked to respond to the survey questions.

The third component examined—via site visits—the innovative approaches being implemented in local agencies. The agencies were selected based upon their responses to a module in the LAS that asked CPS agencies to describe any recent changes in a number of key areas related to operation and functions of CPS. Qualitative interview protocols were used to obtain data from CPS staff and other allied agencies, as appropriate.

Findings

Nearly one-half of all states reported that they had policies providing for an alternative response that did not require making a determination of whether or not maltreatment had occurred. These responses were typically applied to only a subset of referrals and the options were not always available in all counties in a state. The local agency survey revealed that approximately two-thirds of local agencies had an alternative to investigation. Thus alternative responses are being practiced more often than has been previously assumed.[3]

---

2 The reports from this study are available from the National Clearinghouse on Child Abuse and Neglect Information http://www.calib.com/nccanch/ and on the Internet at http://aspe.hhs.gov/hsp/cps-status03.

3 For 2001, 11 States reported that they had a disposition that corresponded to "alternative response victim" or "alternative response nonvictim" (DHHS, *Child Maltreatment 2001*, 2003). The *Literature review* found 10 States had implemented alternative response options that were discussed in academic publications and government reports.

The key questions concerning alternative response that were addressed by the National Study included:

- What are the goals of the alternative response?
- What are the required or commonly conducted activities?
- Are responsibilities coordinated or shared with other agencies?
- What are the qualifications of those who conduct alternative response?
- What new practices are being used to improve the alternative response process?

Alternative response workforce

Only one-fifth of the agencies had specialized workers for the alternative response. In 42% of agencies, workers who conducted an alternative response also conducted screening; in 59% of agencies, alternative response workers also conducted investigations. For all agencies, compared to an average of 43 investigations monthly, an average of 16 alternative responses were completed per month.[4] Because of the overlap in workers, the numbers and qualifications of workers were not very different from the numbers and qualifications of investigation workers.

Goals of alternative response

The overall goals of alternative response approaches were to address low-risk or low-severity situations and, in some cases, to respond to family situations not meeting the mandates for CPS. Only 10 out of 20 states' policies mentioned child safety as the purpose of the alternative response and seven states identified family support and family preservation.

Most policy statements emphasized that the alternative response would be more family-oriented, less threatening or coercive, or more focused on services. Some descriptions of alternative response objectives included the following:

- To provide a response to physical abuse that does not require criminal investigation and allows for services;
- To provide a modified approach for families with low-risk through less threatening community based assessments;
- To facilitate appropriate service responses for families who are not

---

[4] For 2001, approximately 7% of children who received an alternative response were found to be victims of maltreatment in the 11 states that reported on this response to NCANDS (DHHS, *Child Maltreatment 2001*, 2003).

within the required mandate of CPS, but who would benefit from services;
- To provide services without assigning blame; and
- To provide preventive services before a CPS investigation is required.

When available, alternative response options were generally not directed at the more serious types of maltreatment. More than one-half of the agencies providing an alternative response are estimated to exclude moderate or severe physical abuse, moderate or severe sexual abuse, severe neglect, status offenses, or child fatalities from such a response.

Required activities

By and large, the survey of local agencies detected very little difference in the overall set of procedures that workers engage in to complete an alternative response compared to an investigation. Virtually any procedure that was required for investigations could also be conducted as part of an alternative response.

However, workers had more autonomy in deciding what activities to conduct as part of the alternative response compared to the investigation response. As shown in Table 1, even though the activities are the same, a smaller proportion of agencies always performed these activities for alternative response.

Table 1. Investigation and alternative response activities always conducted

Activity	Investigation always	Alternative response always
Interview or formally observe child(ren)	98%	69%
Interview caregiver(s)	98%	73%
Review prior CPS records	89%	80%
Interview witnesses	65%	30%
Interview family members other than caregiver	56%	25%
Remove child harmed or in danger of harm	53%	46%
Obtain/preserve physical evidence	50%	27%
Interview reporter	43%	30%
Interview professional known to family	41%	25%
Visit family without appointment	34%	18%
Conduct criminal background check on alleged perpetrator	32%	23%
Discuss with other CPS workers	24%	19%

The alternative response option was less focused on determining whether maltreatment had occurred, further legal action, or recording information on perpetrators as depicted in Table 2.

Table 2. Procedures in concluding investigation or alternative response

Procedures	Investigation always	Alternative response always
Notify perpetrator	85%	45%
Enter perpetrator in central registry	80%	41%
Notify reporter	30%	21%

Less than one-half of the agencies would always notify a "perpetrator" of the results of an alternative response, compared to 85% of agencies conducting an investigation; approximately one-quarter of agencies would always obtain or preserve physical evidence during an alternative response compared to 50% of agencies conducting an investigation; about one-fifth of agencies would conduct a criminal background check as part of an alternative response compared to about one-third of agencies that would conduct such a check as part of an investigation.

Collaboration and sharing

CPS agencies tend not to assume primary responsibility for maltreatment that is addressed under the alternative response. For example, less than 10% of agencies always had the lead responsibility for all types of maltreatment under alternative response compared to 17% of agencies that always took the lead responsibility for investigation. Law enforcement was also less involved in the alternative response option than it was for investigation. Approximately 39% of agencies shared responsibilities with law enforcement under alternative response compared to 84% of agencies that shared responsibility with law enforcement for investigation.

Barriers and new directions

In general, fewer agencies identified specific barriers they face when conducting an alternative response. Only "predicting what might happen to a child" was found to be an obstacle to completing an alternative response in a timely manner by more than two-thirds of agencies. Given that conducting an alternative response is a relatively new direction for CPS, it is not surprising that few agencies were modifying their assessment approaches. Nine percent of agencies with alternative response had implemented changes in the use of risk assessment or other tools; an additional 9% had considered such changes.

One site visit revealed that the local agency had recently implemented an alternative response appropriate for children who were not in immediate danger. Three factors were used in determining whether an investigation or alternative response would be provided—the severity of the alleged maltreatment, the immediacy of child safety concerns, and overall family needs. The alternative response utilized assessments that focused on family needs and family strengths. Services were provided under this family empowerment model.

Recognition of the need for services in addition to protection and investigation are evident in the widespread inclusion of alternative response services. Study results indicate that, though overlap was evident in the AR and CP services provided, workers were given greater discretion in deciding which services to include in ARS. In general, ARS initiatives sought to provide less intrusive services and to facilitate access to and engagement in services for families with lower risk or lower severity of maltreatment. However, differences were evident across agencies in how alternative responses were implemented in practice. Implicit in the principles of ARS is the assumption that efforts to tailor services to specific child and family needs will yield better outcomes than those achieved with no service or CPS. Outcomes were not evaluated in the first study. However, the second study provides an opportunity to examine rates of engagement and select outcomes for one ARS model.

Washington State evaluation of differential response

Purpose and methods

The objective of the Washington State Alternative Response System (ARS) evaluation was to report on: 1) the general demographics and case characteristics of families referred to ARS services; 2) the type, rate, and frequency of engagement of families in formal and informal services as a result of involvement with ARS services; 3) the safety of children served; and 4) re-referral and placement rates six months post services.

A follow-up of all families referred to ARS programs was conducted. Data from the CPS referral process and re-referral and placement outcomes were collected from the CPS administrative database. Data on ARS engagement and services were collected from the ARS provider.

In 1999, the Washington State Legislature authorized the development of an Alternative Response System, based on diversion of low risk CPS referrals to community based programs. Contracts were developed with 38 agencies statewide to provide assessment and services to low risk families diverted from the CPS system. All families met the criteria for acceptance into the CPS system. A process for identifying each referral to the ARS was developed and ARS contracts included requirements for reporting demographic, case, and outcome data. Initial evaluation of the program revealed a 20% engagement rate of families into service, and a re-referral rate of 28%. The re-referral rates by outcome are as follows: 29% for families who were not served; 27% for families who were assessed but not served; and 28% for those served beyond assessment. About one-half of the re-referrals to CPS occurred within six months. Children in 6% of the families were placed in care after referral to the ARS program. Thirty-three percent of the families with identified substance abuse issues at referral were re-referred and 46% of the families with domestic violence identified at intake were re-referred. The re-referral rate for CPS "business as usual" cases (they were eligible for ARS but there were not enough ARS "slots" available) was 33%.

A follow-up evaluation of the post pilot projects provided additional evaluation data of interest. For the first three years of the project, the service engagement rate was about 20% and during the fourth year, the engagement rate was 50%. However, by the fourth year, payments to the provider were tied to the achievement of service engagement. Examining re-referral data by termination of service reason after six months indicated that 22% of the families assessed as not needing service were re-referred, 29% of the families who refused services, 26% of the families who completed services, and 34% who terminated services for other reasons. Overall the placement rate of families referred to an alternative response was about 6% of referrals.

Conclusions

Alternative response options provide a more textured approach to responding to allegations of maltreatment. These options reflect recognition that adopting a single approach may not be necessary or appropriate given the variety of conditions under the agencies' responsibility. Alternative response services offer the potential for a broader and more flexible set of services to address the needs of children and families who do not meet risk or severity of maltreatment criteria required for CPS services. However, assumptions about how the current CPS system operates and how an alternative model should be structured must be clearly articulated. Clarity and consensus on the nature of risk of harm and appropriate scope for CPS intervention is required before adequate decisions about differential response can be made.

What does the early evaluation data suggest? Advocates for less intrusive services to families argued that families would be more likely to engage. However, redesigning the CPS system may not be a simple matter. Engagement of CPS referred families who have chronic problems (and perhaps mistrust of governmental services) is not an especially easy task. The families in these community based alternative response programs did not overwhelmingly engage. Furthermore, many more families were identified as needing services than received services and the re-referral rate for these families was similar whether they engaged in services or not.

Most CPS agencies decide on the appropriate response option after an initial screening has taken place. Thus, an agency with an alternative response has an increased need for experienced screeners and assessment processes that can accurately differentiate cases based upon risk for re-referral or recurrence. In the Washington State study, risk factors often identified as risk predictors of re-referral were confirmed in this low risk sample. Domestic violence and substance abuse are predictors of re-referral for low and high risk families, whether served by alternative response systems or CPS. This raises the question of whether families who have issues with domestic violence and substance abuse should be referred to voluntary services.

Finally, we should examine whether the current services offered are effective in general or for families with risk factors such as substance abuse and domestic violence. Though the 1994 evaluation documented a more than two-fold increase in engagement rates when payment was attached to service engagement, increased rates of engagement had little impact on re-referral rates among families who received services beyond assessment. These findings also indicate an increased need for good supervision of referral activity, since referral for investigation may be appropriate after an initial alternative response.

It is time to re-examine our service delivery system for at risk and maltreating families. However, rushing to the "cure du jour" without adequately assessing whether that cure actually solves the problem may only exacerbate the problem, rather than fixing it. Research in Washington State would indicate that many families can benefit from a less intrusive response from CPS, whether that is referral to community based agencies or a restructuring of CPS to offer an assessment track. The findings from the Local Agency Survey are also instructive, since they suggest that the greatest barrier to closing alternative response cases is a concern about what will happen to a child. However, the criteria for selection of families for these alternative responses should be based on empirical data that provides information on high vs. low risk.

Most agencies that implement an alternative response do so to address real or perceived limitations associated with the traditional approaches taken to CPS investigations. Alternative responses are intended to provide a less intrusive response to address less serious maltreatment, avoid labeling caretakers as perpetrators, facilitate access to necessary services for families who may be at risk, and to encourage the engagement of families so that they will take advantage of services. Such options receive the most attention as key reforms for CPS because they result in changes in decision making responsibility and different approaches to meeting child and family needs.

Mobilizing communities to prevent child abuse and neglect: A cultural shift in child protection

Liesette Brunson and Camil Bouchard

Abstract

In extending protection for children beyond the minimal child protection that can be afforded by the child welfare system, numerous preventative community based approaches have been implemented across North America. Through illustrations of several community based models, the authors examine strategies for community mobilization. In addition, this chapter raises interesting issues regarding the ways in which community and community interests are defined. Finally, critical elements for community collaboration and some predictable dilemmas are discussed in light of a maximal protection model (Projet Béluga), which is currently being implemented in Montreal neighbourhoods.

From minimal to maximal child protection

Since Quebec implemented its child protection legislation in 1979, community leaders and citizens appear to have implicitly adopted a practice in which reporting suspected cases of maltreatment to the child protection system (CPS) is considered the best, and in fact the only, way to ensure security for children. In other words, child protection is seen as an issue for CPS services exclusively. This reliance on child welfare services to be entirely responsible for child protection could be called a practice of minimal child protection.

Clearly this approach has placed child protection services under intolerable pressure. Reports continue to flow into a system that often only has enough resources to secure the safety of children through the use of court decisions and placements. Clinical interventions aimed at improving family circumstances, investments of time and resources in child development, and attempts to help families meet even basic needs are largely out of reach for protection workers. For example, at least 50% of the families that are reported to Quebec's CPS face very severe economic circumstances. Yet child protection workers tend to ignore these types of economic needs in their recommendations and interventions, partly because they cannot afford the time it takes to access community resources to address these needs, and partly because they do not believe that they can succeed in satisfying these needs (Tourigny et al., 2002).

The pressure on protection workers is exacerbated by a sense of isolation in dealing with their cases (Dagenais, Bastien, Bégin, Bouchard, & Fortin, 2000; Farrow, 1997). Protection services and prevention services are nested in segregated organizations that are each accountable for their own specific mission. Even when official protocols exist to encourage collaboration between protection services and front line prevention services, collaboration is difficult due to lack of time and the absence of facilitating organizational structures. As a result, the tools that are realistically available to CPS workers are often not sufficient to meet families' needs.

Despite the fact that a great deal of resources are dedicated to current child protection systems (Daro & Donelly, 2002), this type of tertiary care system does not appear to have succeeded in improving the situation of children. Recent studies in Ontario and Quebec have demonstrated that number of subtantiated cases of child maltreatment has risen considerably during the last 10 years (Trocmé, Fallon, MacLaurin, & Copp, 2002; Tourigny et al., 2002). In Quebec, despite significant budgetary increases for child protection services, rates of both child neglect and child abuse have continued to rise. In addition, over one-quarter of vulnerable children and families who have been involved with CPS will re-enter the system. This recurrence rate is closely associated with chronic debilitating family conditions such as poverty, and possibly maternal depression, and may reflect the difficulty that CPS workers have in resolving these complex and crystallized situations (Hélie et al., 2002).

This minimal protection, third-line service approach is pervasive in the Quebec system, as it appears to be in most North American systems (Schorr, 1997; Trocmé, Fallon, MacLaurin, and Copp, 2002). Indeed, this approach may be so strongly imprinted on our organizational cultural background that it prevents the emergence of alternatives based on more coherent local leadership and shared accountability for ensuring security for *all* children of the community. In other words, there may be almost no local leadership around the issue of children's security because no one is accountable for the security of all children as opposed to the security of reported children only.

This situation has led to calls for a radical shift to an alternative that installs a strong civic leadership around the issue of protection for all children. In contrast to the minimal child protection approach, this alternative could be called a maximal protection approach. In a maximal protection approach, the fundamental rights of all children to be protected against threats to their physical, psychological and social security are affirmed. These rights, as well as systems to ensure these rights, would be in place to protect children from birth on. These rights would engage every citizen and every relevant organization, program and service in the mission of securing or restoring conditions that ensure the security of all children in their community. Success in protecting each and every child would be the responsibility of all relevant resources of the community and no one would be left alone to ensure child protection. Prevention of problems would be as much of a focus as providing appropriate response when problems occur. Indeed, this approach calls for a cultural shift in child protection, not just within child protection systems, but within society as a whole.

The best research and thinking about the causes of child abuse and neglect support the idea that this type of maximal child protection approach is essential to truly protect children. According to the ecological framework for understanding and preventing child maltreatment (Belsky, 1993; Garbarino & Kostelny, 1992), threats to children's security are numerous and are nested in a large diversity of systems. Research has documented multiple risks and protective factors that are related to child maltreatment (Belsky, 1993; Coulton, Korbin, Su, & Chow, 1995; Garbarino & Sherman, 1980; Garbarino & Kostelny, 1992; Sampson, 2001; Sampson, Raudenbush, & Earls, 1997). These findings suggest that to be effective in providing maximal protection for each and every child, communities must have all of their relevant resources and services committed to this effort.

This appeal for a more integrated preventive, community based approach to child protection is certainly not new (see Farrow, 1997). However, this task is neither easy nor simple. A paradigm shift is never accomplished overnight and its proponents certainly need not be embarrassed by repeating the same plea over and over again. This is unavoidable in any important paradigmatic shift (Kuhn, 1968).

Example programs

In trying to build leadership around the issue of maximal child protection, inspiration can be drawn from examples of demonstration projects and community trials that have worked to specifically target the prevention of child maltreatment using a comprehensive, community based approach. In her remarkable book, *Common purpose*, Schorr (1997) offers a number of inspiring illustrations of local and regional initiatives aimed at reinforcing the protection blanket for children. For example, in the Los Angeles region, 25 local networks have been put into place in neighbourhoods with the highest incidence of children removed from home as a result of maltreatment. Evaluations of some of these efforts report a decrease in out-of-home placement by a third over a period of three years (Schorr, 1997, p. 219).

Another program, Building Community Partnerships for Child Protection, seeks to enhance the ability of communities to protect children from abuse and neglect by engaging a broad range of stakeholders—from government agencies to non-profit groups to local community residents—in assuming responsibility for child safety (Schorr, 1997). This initiative addresses child abuse and neglect through a variety of interrelated strategies: raising neighbourhood awareness of child safety issues, empowering neighbourhood residents to become more involved with families at risk of abusing or neglecting their children, strengthening locally based organizations and helping them to form networks concerned with child safety, and fostering policy, practice, and organizational changes within public sector child protective services agencies. Within this broad framework, local communities develop their own strategies tailored to the local community. For example, in Iowa, the Cedar Rapids patch approach borrows from a long-standing British intervention tradition, in which diverse services are co-located under the same roof in the neighbourhood. Workers work together to provide integrated services to address a variety of possible family needs. Families are welcome to walk in to local centres to meet with members of the patch team who assist them with a large variety of issues, such as housing, employment, and health, education, and child development. Members of the patch team, in which one also finds CPS workers, learn to deal with concerns that would not be theirs otherwise, and so become familiar with local resources. They also are able to negotiate services and support for families with community resources and to identify common elements in the various stresses encountered by the families (Adams & Krauth, 1995).

While these partnerships can take many forms, several ingredients seem to be universal. First, the CPS worker is one member of a larger, multi-sectorial local coalition. Second, this local coalition ensures that customized services are available to support parents well before child protection services are needed. Third, the entry point to this support system is moved ahead from the CPS to more preventive programs or services. Fourth, intensive and diversified interventions are offered to reported families. Finally, economic and environmental factors are also examined in an attempt to reinforce the most important protection system around the child: the family. Thus, community development corporations and other economically oriented programs can also be seen as making important contributions to the maximal protection of local children.

These types of partnerships are based on the recognition that a large variety of community resources must work together for a maximal protection outcome. Their goal is to develop a more coherent local leadership based on shared accountability for ensuring the security of all children in our communities. Much more is going on than just adding and coordinating services. These initiatives are building a strong local capacity for change and improving the ways that all children are protected by all sectors of the community (Hogan, 1999).

This type of shared accountability cannot exist in a vacuum. It has to rest on strong local collaboration and mobilization grounded in a vision of maximal child protection shared by all involved partners. To achieve a strong and sustainable collaboration, local organizational structures have to be created or activated that have the role of coordinating and integrating local efforts to achieve maximal child protection.

Key elements for success in community mobilization

In order to work towards the goal of maximal child protection in Quebec, a program of community mobilization entitled *Projet Béluga* is currently being developed for implementation in a small number of Montreal neighbourhoods. Reviewing example programs such as those described above has identified some core elements that appear to be critical for this type of mobilization, as well as some predictable dilemmas that similar mobilization efforts have had to face.

Multi-sector coalition committed to working together towards maximal child protection

The first key element in a comprehensive, community based approach to maximal protection for all children is an organizational structure that coordinates collaboration among partners committed to working together toward this goal. This coalition provides local leadership around this issue by ensuring coordination among existing services and programs, identifying and developing new services and programs that can address the full range of family needs, and working towards changing the broader neighbourhood environment to be more supportive of families.

Although these partnership structures can vary in terms of shapes and rules, they should embrace all resources that could contribute to efficiently and respectfully supporting parents in their daily challenges of parenting before the family system becomes overloaded and dysfunctional. The partners must include health and social services (including CPS[1]), but also schools, employment services, continuing education, parental education services, mental health services, recreational and respite resources, housing, transportation, university researchers, as well as banking, financing, and retailing businesses. These partners must be committed to the common vision of creating a community that provides maximal protection for all children and to providing local leadership to implement this vision.

Data orientation

A second key element for a comprehensive, community based approach is a willingness to look at and learn from locally relevant benchmarking data that provide information about the community's current situation, as well as about coalition activities and impacts. For example, on the basis of an already strong state tradition of community collaboration, the state of Vermont has developed an approach to a maximal child protection system in which local partnerships rely on stable and repeated measures of outcomes (indicators) to inspire their action plan and to make necessary changes to existing plans. This data-oriented approach gathers people of the community around the same data so that they can share the same concerns and can look in the same direction (Hogan, 1999). As Hogan (1999) has stated, "Indicators are the tool with which we take our bearings, chart and correct our course, and monitor conditions around us on an ongoing basis" (p. 11). In other words, data help the coalition to stay focused.

The benefits of using indicators are certainly compelling (Hogan, 1999). Stable indicators protect decision-making against shifting conditions of public policy, economic and social trends, and political rhetoric. In addition, data give local coalitions a sense of the distance that has been covered by the community, of how well the community stands as compared to others, and of how much community efforts have paid off. They also provide motivation for self-improvement, can help build more political support around the collective community actions, and connect better with the business community (Hogan, 1999). Indicators are also easily communicated through the local media, potentially facilitating broader awareness and mobilization around the targeted issues.

---

1 Daro and Darrow (2002) have cautioned that prevention programs too often position themselves as alternatives to the child protection system, rather than working together with CPS. CPS must be an important partner in the coalition as well as in the field, working to deliver neighbourhood based services.

In Canada, the Vancouver Human Early Learning Partnership (HELP) heavily relies on geo-mapping and indicators for sustaining a strong community commitment toward Vancouver children (Hertzman, McLean, Kohen, Dunn, & Evans, 2002). Their work has documented how institutional resources can vary dramatically across neighbourhoods, with the poorest neighbourhoods, where need is greatest, often having fewer resources. Another data-oriented effort is a simple but sophisticated web based geo-mapping system (CAN-DO) developed by the Cleveland Community Building Initiative. This system is capable of informing local partnerships about the state of the various family risks and of their interactions (Center on Urban Poverty and Social Change, n.d.). Data based tools such as these help local coalitions stay focused, assess progress, and communicate effectively to the local community and broader audiences.

Evidence based strategies

A third key element of a comprehensive, community based approach to child protection is the provision of evidence based strategies and programs. Weber (1998) argues for conceptualizing the services necessary for child protection as running the gamut from primary prevention to therapeutic response, including: 1) universal services for all families to assist with positive, effective, nurturing parenting; 2) prevention with at-risk families; 3) early intervention at first signs of behaviour; 4) crisis response to deal with abuse; and 5) therapeutic response to deal with consequences of abuse. Currently, the majority of child protection resources are devoted to the child protection system's efforts to provide tertiary care in terms of crisis response and therapeutic response. Relatively fewer resources are provided for universal promotion, targeted prevention, or early intervention services. Further, even when these resources are present, they are rarely coordinated and integrated with child protection systems, or even easily available to CPS.

Thus, local coalitions will likely take on the task of developing and coordinating a diversity of early, voluntary, holistic family support services. These promotion and prevention oriented services should be holistic in supporting parents in their role of parenting and in meeting a diversity of family needs (Bethea, 1999). Traditional family support services should be made more available to strengthen parents' parenting and family management skills, addressing issues such as appropriate discipline, knowledge of child development, nutrition and feeding problems, safety issues, time management, budgeting, and stress management and coping. Emergency support should be available for parents 24 hours a day through telephone hotlines or warmlines and respite care centres (Bethea, 1999). In addition, these services should also address concerns such as jobs, food security, and housing, which are too often considered outside the range of promotion and prevention programs dedicated to child well-being. However, until a parent's basic needs are met, they may find it difficult to meet the needs of their children (Bethea, 1999). Thus, needs for food, shelter, clothing, safety, and medical and dental care, the resolution of spousal abuse, treatment for alcohol and drug abuse, financial concerns, and employment and legal problems must all be addressed. These services should be universally available and voluntary, although more intensive services should also be made available to families in higher risk situations (possibly requiring screening processes and case management).

Not only should services be diverse and comprehensive, the local system should be coordinated and integrated so that families who request one type of service find it easier to access a diverse range of services to meet their individual situation. Families should be able to enter the system from multiple entry points and obtain access to comprehensive, coordinated services that respond to their individual situations. Further, these services should be available before the onset of severe family crisis, so that children do not have to be hurt before families receive support (Bethea, 1999).

In addition to implementing reforms in local service delivery systems, coalitions targeting maximal child protection may also undertake strategies to change the neighbourhood milieu to be more supportive of families. One common approach to this goal is a social marketing campaign designed to influence local beliefs, attitudes, norms, and behaviour regarding child protection. This type of campaign can communicate and reinforce appropriate responses that community organizations and individuals can take. For example, Weber (1998) argues every sector can play an effective role regarding child abuse. Religious institutions can promote value systems that treasure children, as well as the opportunity for parents to break out of their social isolation; individuals can provide positive contact, social support, and informal mentoring to families in difficulty. Other approaches to changing the neighbourhood milieu could include encouraging the development of a diversity of settings where parents and children can gather, interact, support, and learn from each other. Coalitions might also support organizations working at the grassroots level to organize residents and to address economic and social inequities that disproportionately affect vulnerable families and contribute to their vulnerability (Hyman, 2002; Kordesh, 1995).

Parent/citizen input

Services and programs adopted by local coalitions should be evidence based as much as possible, and certainly accountable to high standards. At the same time, the emphasis on evidence based strategies should remain flexible enough to facilitate innovation and local adaptation because we know that not every service or program works in every context. The prevention science approach (Roosa, Jones, Tein, & Cree, 2003) of using data and evidence based strategies may be powerful tools, but flexibility and responsiveness to community needs and to community input are also essential (Schorr, 1997). In fact, a prevention science approach could actually be more of a hindrance than an asset if it ignores the importance of family and community participation (Brunson, Bouchard, & Larrivée, 2003; Himmelman, 2001).

A significant and meaningful role for parents is essential in ensuring families' abilities to provide maximal child protection for their own children and for all children of the community. Bethea (1999) has argued that in order to be truly successful in enhancing families' abilities to protect and care for their children, prevention programs must enhance parents' ability to foster optimal development of their children and themselves, must treat parents as vital contributors to their children's health and development, and must create opportunities for parents to feel empowered to act on their own behalf and behalf of their children. Coalitions that facilitate and are responsive to parent input and participation can support this parent and family empowerment process. This approach is critical, and should be supported by coalition efforts in terms of coalition process and community input as well as by service provision and neighbourhood improvement.

In addition, community input and responsiveness to community concerns are also essential for local success. As Schorr, Sylvester, and Dunkle (1999) have argued, "Effective neighbourhood transformation requires that outsiders draw on information, expertise and wisdom than can come from the neighbourhood itself and that community based organizations be able to draw on funding, expertise and influence from outside."[2] Perhaps one does not need to choose between a top-down and a bottom-up

---

[2] Alan Pence, from the University of Victoria, when asked to work on a child care training program by a North Saskatchewan Aboriginal chief, answered that he did not know anything about Aboriginal culture and that he was not the appropriate resource for them. The Chief replied, "This is exactly why we ask you: you know about child care, we know about our people" (Dahlberg, Moss, & Pence, 1999). Since then Pence has experienced what he calls the "power of not knowing" and has developed with Aboriginal communities customized child care training programs relying on both scientific and vernacular knowledge, the First Nations Partnership Programs (Ball & Pence, 1999).

approach or, as described by Himmelman (2001), between a betterment and an empowerment approach. Instead, mixing these strategies may permit both the scientific community and the local community to bring their own original knowledge to the planning and creation of maximally secure environments for all children (Brunson et al., 2003).

Predictable dilemmas in community mobilization

In addition to identifying key elements of success in comprehensive, community based approaches to child protection, it is also important to identify some of the common dilemmas and challenges these efforts may face. Daro and Donnelly (2002) have warned us that prevention programs for child maltreatment have consistently overstated their potential and misrepresented the type of families that voluntary prevention programs are able and likely to reach. It is therefore important to examine and learn from some of the constraints and dilemmas previous innovators in the field have experienced.

How to mobilize the community

One important dilemma previous programs have faced is how to get people involved and mobilized. This is a question of how to create energy that spurs mobilization. On the one hand, using numbers, rates, and maps can enhance community readiness by creating a sense of urgency to act. However, emphasizing that a neighbourhood or a family is at risk for child abuse and neglect is potentially stigmatizing (Godenzi & Depuy, 2001). Focusing on weaknesses and needs has also been criticized for reinforcing a deficiency model, for failing to recognize and build on individual and communities' existing strengths, and for having to potential to further stigmatize and marginalize disadvantaged groups (Kordesh, 1995; Kretzmann & McKnight, 1993; McKnight, 1987). Further, it is not clear whether highlighting weaknesses and vulnerabilities is an effective way to engage families.

In public health strategic planning, a common alternative to this deficiency model is to revert to a promotional, non-threatening mode in which goals are couched in positive pro-developmental and well-being terms. Unfortunately, it may be harder to mobilize people without a sense of urgency or threat. Take the example of forest protection: we are more motivated and more easily mobilized to take action to preserve our forests when we believe that our own quality of life, or the quality of life for our children is directly at stake. Similarly, past experience with a Montreal promotional initiative (1, 2, 3 GO!) suggests that community mobilization can be harder to achieve without the presence of a threat (Bouchard, 1999). Further, a promotional stance could potentially backfire on a community, if it reinforces a collective denial of a real threat that exists to the community's children.

Two strategies may be useful in attempting to create energy for mobilization without further marginalizing vulnerable families. One strategy may be to broaden the size of the neighbourhood being mobilized. Neighbourhoods that are too small are easy to identify and single out. Further, small, disadvantaged areas do not usually contain sufficient resources to support an effective mobilization effort. Larger living areas such as France's arrondissements are large enough to nest various neighbourhood profiles. These larger areas also are more likely to contain resources and capacities that are not already overtaxed.

A second strategy may be to use a problem analysis (Biglan & Taylor, 2000) that places emphasis on environmental factors that contribute to breakdowns in families' abilities to protect their children. For example, Garbarino's (1995) work on socially toxic environments suggests that there are multiple toxic agents that hinder parents from fulfilling the ultimate protective function for their children. These toxic agents include chronic exposure to actual violence or social norms that promote violence, social marginalization or isolation, lack of community resources; chronic poverty, instability; inadequate housing, and other similar threats.

In developing an approach to community mobilization around child protection in Montreal, we are exploring whether this conceptualization of a toxic environment can be used to place emphasis on the contextual factors that contribute to breakdowns in families' ability to protect their children. A powerful analogy that could help accomplish this shift in focus may be to draw a parallel between vulnerable parents and the situation of beluga whales in the St. Lawrence River. These whales are literally forced to swallow large quantities of poisons that have been disgorged by aluminium mills and other polluting sources into the river environment and the Quebec people have become strongly mobilized to address these threats to the belugas. Thus, Projet Béluga rests on the conviction is that this analogy can help to raise consciousness about the devastating environments some parents have to face daily to create collective empathy and sympathy for these parents and to mobilize community assets in fighting those toxic agents.

What is the role of local community residents?

Another important dilemma that previous prevention programs have experienced is in defining who to get involved and mobilized in the effort to create maximal child protection. Neighbourhoods can be described in terms of organizations and services that are located there, and that is clearly one appropriate focus of mobilization efforts. However, efforts to rally natural neighbourhood support networks and to change local social norms are often less successful in mobilizing local residents in ways that change these informal social relationships.

One possible reason for this relative lack of success could be a tendency to assume that the informal social relationships in local neighborhoods are cohesive and unified; in other words, that there is a cohesive community present in the targeted neighbourhood. Indeed, there is quite often a tendency to refer to a local neighbourhood as a unitary entity: "the community." Unfortunately, this reference may lead to oversimplified assumptions about the complexities of neighbourhood and community life. Referring to neighbourhoods and communities synonymously may imply that just because a group of individuals or families happen to share geographic space, there is automatically a cohesive community unifying them. This reference may also suggest that there is only one group, one set of interests, and one voice in the neighbourhood. Finally, this reference may lead to the assumption that local institutions and organizations are capable of representing the interests of all community members in an unproblematic, uncontested way. These may be oversimplified assumptions about neighbourhood and community life that can have negative consequences for the process of mobilizing community residents.

It is certainly true that some neighbourhoods are characterized by cohesive social relations. When social cohesion and collective efficacy characterize a neighbourhood, they have been found to be strong protective factors against social problems such as delinquency and child maltreatment (Sampson, 2001; Garbarino & Kostelny, 1992; Garbarino & Sherman, 1980).

Where substantial cohesion exists in urban neighbourhoods despite impoverishment, these dynamics should be treasured and facilitated. However, it is also important to recognize that many neighborhoods may have few social networks, little social capital, and few trusted informal social relationships, and that they may be characterized by disengagement, alienation, and even conflict rather than social cohesion. Neighbours in these types of disordered neighbourhoods have often withdrawn from neighbourhood life for very compelling reasons, not necessarily just because they lack a catalyst to be involved (Brodsky, 1996; Stack, 1997). Even though these dynamics likely contribute to families' vulnerability, it may be difficult to create cohesive relations where there is currently anomie and distrust, unless there are also changes in the conditions which structure and shape those relationships.

Thus, it may be important to avoid overestimating or overstating the potential that social marketing or service provision and reforms might have to build communities, transform informal social dynamics, build democratic institutions, and create community where currently there is none. To the extent that informal social dynamics can be shaped by intervention efforts, this process is likely to take place through grass-roots organizing efforts working for neighbourhood transformation (Kordesh, 1995).[3] Coalitions that seek to change informal social relationships and local social norms should support these types of direct strategies for building social capital among resident groups (e.g., Hyman, 2002).

Collaborations are difficult

Finally, even internally to the coalition, coalitions can run across predictable dilemmas. Collaborative partnerships can be difficult and they require careful planning, support, and monitoring, as well as adequate staff time and training. Daro and Donnelley (2002) point out that it takes considerable time to learn how to work together across service models and program areas. Some of the predictable issues that must often be addressed include fears about liability and accountability, categorical funding streams that limit who can receive services, communication channels between organizations, fiscal and caseload pressures, bureaucratic inertia, and risk avoidance (Waldfogel, 2001a). The time and effort involved in building and maintaining these relationships and communication patterns are most often underestimated. Further, a huge amount of time is required to recruit and train new members and leaders, to build shared understanding and consensus, to resolve conflicts, to deal with turnover, and to decide on and implement appropriate action steps. Appropriate time, resources, and support should be devoted to facilitating these internal dynamics to ensure coalition success.

Conclusion

There are no simple answers to these dilemmas, as there are no simple answers in dealing with a complex social problem like child maltreatment. However, the time is ripe for installing a new paradigm of maximal pro-

---

3 Kordesh (1995) and McKnight (1988) have argued that organizations focused on service delivery should be cautious in trying to take on the work of more informal, grassroots organizations and movements. These more powerful and resource-rich institutional entities certainly have an extremely important role in encouraging grassroots efforts and in providing services and resources that complement grassroots efforts. Furthermore, existing grassroots organizations should certainly be included in coalitions focused on community mobilization. However, Kordesh (1995) argues compellingly that service systems should support and facilitate grassroots organizations as independent entities, rather than trying to take on this work themselves.

tection for children in our communities—a paradigm based on children's fundamental rights and parent support. Some key elements and models for this new paradigm are already in place and many others with great potential have been identified. But more than that is needed. The task now is to match these paradigmatic assets with local and national political leadership. In 1998, the Quebec government sponsored a task force to examine the entire issue of child protection in the communities. The resulting Cliche Report (1998) stressed the importance of establishing collaboration among all local and regional organizations. Ministerial plans have followed and confirmed this orientation and networks of local community (preventive) services and of protection services have worked together to identify the necessary ingredients of such complicity and have contracted each other in the pursuit of more integrated services. Broader community mobilization could support and enhance these efforts. This chapter has described some of the foundations of an approach to community mobilization around the issue of maximal child protection that is currently being developed in Montreal. There is hope these combined efforts to establish maximal child protection will contribute to providing all children with the maximal protection that every child deserves.

Community based child welfare services in Guelph and Wellington County

Maurice D. Brubacher and Jasma Narayan

Abstract

The provision of services to children and families in need at the Family and Children's Services of Guelph and Wellington County is based on the belief that child protection is a community responsibility. As such, the agency strives to mobilize community resources to protect children, assist families in difficulty, and provide care for children. Through an illustration of the Shelldale Centre, which brings 16 agencies and community organizations together to meet the needs of high-risk children and families, the components of a successful community based service model are described. Child-centred interventions, in which the parents and service providers act as partners and provide outreach to families most in need, are key components of the sucesses achieved by the Shelldale Centre. Positive outcomes for parents and children, as well as significant improvements in neighbourhood safety have been identified. Finally, positive and significant impacts on child welfare services have been observed. Referrals are made earlier and more children are protected within their own homes, which decrease the number of children that need to be placed in care. Overall, the experience in Guelph and Wellington County suggests that children, families, communities, and service providers can benefit substantially from community based child welfare services.

The community based service model

Family and Children's Services of Guelph and Wellington County (F&CS) believes that child protection is a total community responsibility and that mandated services are best provided within a community based service model. The agency strives to mobilize community resources to protect children, assist families in difficulty, and provide care for children.

Commitment to the community based model is reflected in the agency's mission statement:

> Our mission is to provide for the protection of children. Together with others, we will support and encourage families and promote caring communities that share responsibility for the well-being of all children.

F&CS has a community based structure through which services to families are provided at the local level, while residential care and administrative services are centralized. The service model includes a range of child protection interventions and a variety of creative community partnerships. Foster parents, volunteers, and adopting families are key partners in supporting families and protecting children within the community. Other community resources include extended family and informal support systems, community agencies, schools, heath care services, municipalities, recreation programs, and faith groups. Intake and family services are organized into geographic teams that are located at the community level and, where possible, co-located with other community services.

When F&CS services and staff are well known at the local level, child protection concerns and requests for assistance are often made earlier, when interventions can prevent more serious child protection issues and the need for admissions of children into agency care. Similarly, these relationships ensure that other community resources are more accessible to children and families.

When a child has been identified as being in need of protection, community based case management can make maximum use of community resources to help the family resolve the protection issues. Community based case management can assist the family to strengthen relationships with extended family members, to access other community agency services and get the children involved in community programs, and to link with informal community and neighbourhood resources.

F&CS also provides an in-home family support program and trained community volunteers to assist families to address identified child protection issues. Parent-aides provide practical and emotional help to parents who are struggling with parenting responsibilities. Special friends are matched with vulnerable, high-risk, and troubled children and youth and volunteer drivers provide transportation for clients to attend essential appointments and programs.

As much as possible, the agency seeks to resolve child protection issues on a voluntary basis. Alternatives to apprehension and court involvement are seen as preferable except in cases of serious child maltreatment or situations of serious safety issues. The agency prefers to use mediative strategies and voluntary service agreements whenever possible.

When a child cannot be protected within the family, F&CS workers will work with the family to facilitate placement for the child with extended family members, friends or another family known to the child whenever this is possible and appropriate. Such community based kinship care and private placements are less disruptive and stigmatizing for the child than being placed into foster care. Such placements also allow for greater continuity of care for the child and do not require parents to relinquish guardianship of the child in order to get the assistance that they may require to get through a difficult time.

Some children do need to be placed in F&CS care for their protection. For these children, F&CS is committed to providing foster care within the community whenever possible. Foster care is a local community resource for children in care that is preferred over placement in outside group care settings. Similarly, when children in care cannot be returned home, F&CS is committed to permanency planning and placement into adoptive families whenever possible. The agency maintains strong foster care and post adoption support programs. Through extensive networking, community education, and recruitment programs, the agency has had ongoing success in recruiting adequate numbers of high quality local foster families.

As a major community service agency, F&CS takes a lead responsibility in influencing the development of an integrated children's services system. Within the Shared Services and Service Resolution program, agency partners and families come together in search of creative solutions to complex and challenging issues. These agency partners include mental health services, developmental services, health care services, neighbourhood groups, school boards, violence against women programs, counselling services, and others. The agency has active service protocols with these agencies. F&CS also plays a lead role in advocating for additional community services that are required to serve children at risk and children in need of protection.

Some years ago, F&CS established the Children's Foundation of Guelph and Wellington. This is now an independent organization dedicated to raising funds in support of vulnerable children. Programs provided by the Foundation include sponsorship of participation in summer camp and recreation programs, post secondary school scholarships for vulnerable children and youth, and the Adopt-A-Family program that provides Christmas food and gifts for children and families.

F&CS also plays a lead role in the development of neighbourhood primary prevention programs, including family support, outreach, recreation, food support, and community development. Together with the City of Guelph and the Guelph Community Health Centre, F&CS sponsors the Guelph Neighbourhood Support Coalition and its member groups that offer these programs in local neighbourhoods. F&CS is also the umbrella transfer payment agency for the Onward Willow Better Beginnings, Better Futures program.

The Shelldale Centre: A Village of Support

The community based model is well illustrated by the Shelldale Centre: A Village of Support. At Shelldale, 16 agencies and community organizations have come together under F&CS leadership to meet the needs of high-risk children and families. At the centre of this network is the neighbourhood based primary prevention program called Onward Willow Better Beginnings, Better Futures (BBBF). BBBF provides early years programs, family support and outreach, children and youth programs, and community development services.

The components of the community based service model have come together in unique and exciting ways within the Shelldale Centre. Shelldale is a former elementary school facility situated within the Onward Willow neighbourhood, being the area in Guelph that has the highest rates of poverty and family problems. It is also an area where many new immigrant and refugee families settle initially upon arriving in Canada.

The Shelldale Centre provides offices and space for programs, meetings, and activities for 16 partner organizations and community groups. These partners provide programs in the following areas:

- Onward Willow Better Beginnings, Better Futures primary prevention
- Child, youth and family recreation
- Early childhood programs
- Adult education and employment training
- Mental health services and family counselling
- Community policing and victim services
- Violence against women support programs
- Family health
- Developmental services
- Child welfare services

The Shelldale Centre's mission is to provide a seamless network of formal agencies, community organizations, and neighbourhood groups that are mutually committed to serving the needs of children, youth, families, and individuals in the Onward Willow neighbourhood and the larger West Guelph area. The mandate of the Centre is derived from the joint commitment of partner organizations. The Centre is based on a belief in the strength of citizen participation and leadership in identifying local needs and participating in decisions that affect their lives. Partners are committed to innovative programs and structures that will best serve the needs of the community and support the partner organizations in fulfilling our shared vision.

The former school was purchased by F&CS with assistance from the City of Guelph. Initial funds were provided by the F&CS Capital Fund, the Ontario Ministry of Community, Family and Children's Services, partner organizations, and local service clubs. The Shelldale Centre is now owned and operated by Shelldale Centres Incorporated, an independent corporation affiliated with F&CS.

Ongoing guidance and direction to the Shelldale Centre is provided by the Shelldale Centre Coordinator and working groups and committees of the partner organizations. Through the Shelldale Partners group, agency partners and neighbourhood leaders come together to make decisions in the overall best interests of the Centre and its members.

Onward Willow Better Beginnings, Better Futures

The Onward Willow Better Beginnings, Better Futures (BBBF) Family Centre occupies a major portion of the Shelldale Centre. The Better Beginnings, Better Futures programs include four well integrated components with approximately 600-700 families as active participants, including 200 children under five years of age and 300 children over five years of age who attend programs regularly. Families attending BBBF speak 27 different languages, so translation is routinely provided.

While Family and Children's Services is the sponsoring agency, there is an autonomous BBBF Board of Directors comprised of 14 community members and eight service providers. F&CS has an appointed seat on the Board to provide for maximum stability and flexibility.

Figure 1 depicts how the child is the at the centre of all work that is done in the neighbourhood. This picture has been a powerful symbol of hope throughout the neighbourhood. The BBBF model nests programs for children within programs for families, all of whom have access to neighbourhood supports run by the Onward Willow Neighbourhood Group. Service providers are seen as partners with resources to help families.

Figure 1: Child focused, family centred, and community based model

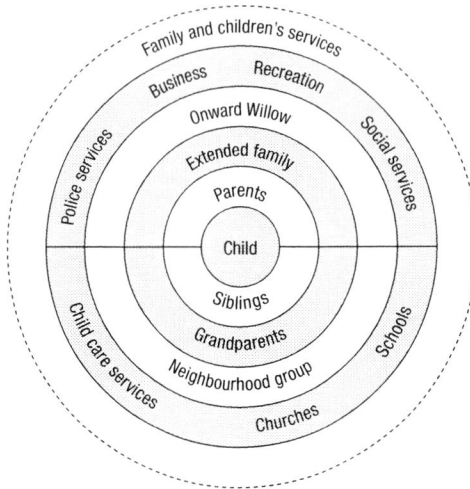

Integration of services is the art of blending program ingredients and respectful relationships across the full spectrum including community members, families in difficulty, and agency staff, managers and executive directors. Within the BBBF program, community residents are seen as citizens, program participants, and potential leaders—and not as clients. Moms, dads and grandparents are treated as consultants and advisors, as well as participants. Service providers are seen as partners and helpers rather than as controllers and owners. To achieve this, there is an ongoing process of learning, training, mentoring, coaching, practicing skills, and supporting community leaders.

Community leaders include current and former F&CS client parents. Many are single moms, many have chronic depression and other mental illnesses, and some are new immigrants and refugees with fresh memories of rape and ethnic cleansing. Almost every woman has experienced violence and abuse in her life. Most families cannot feed their children three times a day for the whole month. While these families are usually classified as hard-to-reach, within BBBF they are the core participants. A key success of the program is the outreach to these families and sustaining their involvement over time.

At the community level, the Onward Willow Neighbourhood Group maintains a wonderful informal network of supports for families that are accessible and available upon request. These include free clothing, emergency food packages, community events, and neighbour-to-neighbour help. Community leaders and volunteers contribute over 20,000 hours of time every year to the programs. In addition to concrete supports, community leaders experience a deep sense of personal meaning, a sense of belonging, and the experience that helping others is a part of the healing process. Active conflict is usually seen as a positive route to consensus, compromise and creative resolution to challenging problems.

Evaluation results within the Onward Willow neighbourhood point to reductions in youth crime, improved neighbourhood safety, better school performance, and improved family functioning as the result of primary prevention, community development, and agency partnerships. The Shelldale Centre has been, and continues to be, instrumental in improving relationships between agencies and promoting interagency referrals and collaborative services.

There are many positive outcomes for parents. Many have gained the confidence to return to school, find well paying jobs, and/or become self-employed. Parents help to plan, implement, and evaluate all programs. Parents provide formal and informal child care. Some have become approved foster parents. Others teach English to immigrant friends and organize community events.

Programs and outcomes for children are especially heart-warming. Baby days and early infant development groups are available for all. Every child from infancy to kindergarten can participate in an appropriate play group. School aged children have access to a daily breakfast club, recreation programs, and summer day camps. As a result, neighbourhood children are better prepared for future success. The local school reports that the BBBF programs have resulted in higher literacy skills and increased attentiveness at the point of school entry. Academic performance has improved and there are fewer social and behavioural problems. (Ontario Association of Children's Aid Societies, 2002).

Partnerships with service providers are very strong. Within the Shelldale Centre, many helpful relationships are established between community residents and agency staff. The umbrella function of F&CS is critical to the success of Better Beginnings. Agency partners provide a wide range of supports including staff expertise, administrative support, gifts in kind, board and committee participation, and ongoing consultation. As a result of these effective partnerships, agency interventions are experienced as less intrusive and more helpful. Early identification of family problems and early intervention are more possible. When child protection issues are identified, there is a full range of neighbourhood resources to draw upon, including family supports, informal caregivers, and neighbourhood programs.

BBBF program evaluations have demonstrated that an integrated program model of primary prevention is especially effective in producing positive outcomes for children and rekindling a strong sense of community, as well as being a cost effective investment to benefit vulnerable children and families and the broader community.

Impact on child welfare services

A positive and high profile for F&CS within the community ensures that community members and professionals are more likely to make early referrals of child protection concerns. As well, they are more likely to be willing to work collaboratively with F&CS as partners in helping to address the identified protection issues.

Through the community based service model, more community resources are available to support children and families in difficulty. As a result, more children can be protected within their own families, without the need for admissions into F&CS care. Private placements provide for less intrusive interventions when children cannot remain at home.

Similarly, foster care and adopting families can be more easily recruited and supported. Thus, there is less need for outside purchased group care placements and children in care can be placed closer to home and can often continue to attend local community schools.

When compared with other agency service patterns (Ontario Association of Children's Aid Societies, 2002), F&CS has consistently shown a low rate of children in care, a low rate of group care placements and a high rate of adoption placements. Figures 2, 3 and 4 show how F&CS service results compare in relation to provincial, regional, and local zone averages. (The Grand River Zone is a geographical group of agencies from the Niagara region in the south to Grey County in the north, and west of Toronto to the Waterloo region. It is an area larger than the ministry's Central West region and includes some of the agencies within that region.) In each case, F&CS results are significantly favourable. F&CS also shows a high rate of private placements and relatively low rates of client legal costs. Interestingly, in the Onward Willow neighbourhood, the rate of children in care per 100 open family services cases was 22% lower than that of F&CS.[1]

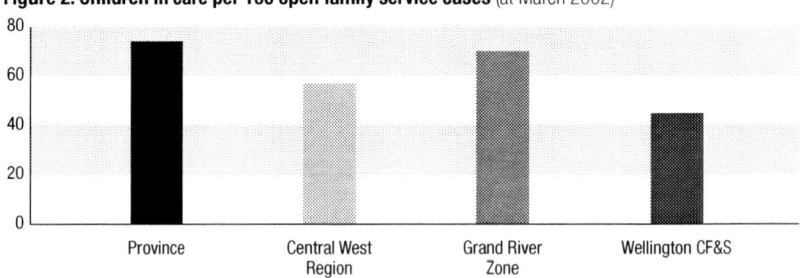

Figure 2. Children in care per 100 open family service cases (at March 2002)

---

1   Internal agency data comparisons, June 2003.

Figure 3. Number of days in group care as percentage of total number of in-care days
(2001–2002)

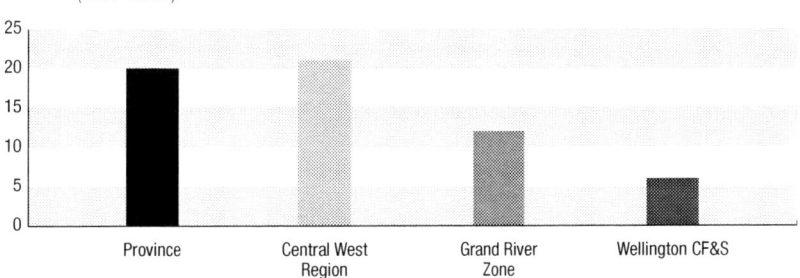

Figure 4. Number of days on adoption probation as percentage of total number of all in-care days
(2001–2002)

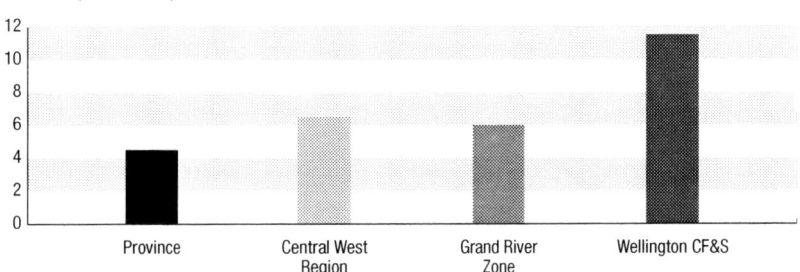

More specifically, if F&CS service patterns had been similar to the Ontario Association of Children's Aid Societies' Central West Region average in 2001-2002, the agency would have had 94 more children in care, 45 more children placed in group care, and 15 fewer adoption placements. If the provincial funding framework was applied, this would have generated additional funding eligibility of more than $7 million. This represents substantial cost savings, considering that the agency's total expenditures for the year were $11 million.[2]

From this experience, it is evident that the F&CS community based service model produces quality child protection services at substantially reduced costs. Children, families, and neighbourhoods benefit substantially from effective community partnerships and community based services.

---

[2] These conclusions are drawn by comparing F&CS service patterns to regional service patterns and calculating the funding allocation to which F&CS would have been eligible had the agency had numbers of children in care and group care placements that were similar to regional averages, based on data drawn from the *Funding and services analysis* of Ontario Association of Children's Aid Societies (2002).

Alberta Response Model: Transforming outcomes for children and youth

Suzanne Anselmo, Russ Pickford, and Phil Goodman

Abstract

The Alberta Response Model (ARM) is based on the principle that protecting children, preventing maltreatment, and strengthening families form a service continuum. ARM retains as a fundamental objective providing protection to children at risk for future maltreatment. However, within this model, children identified as lower risk, whose families are willing to work at solving their own problems, are no longer left to manage with few supports. ARM is comprised of four inter-related core strategies. First, a differential response will ensure children and youth at high risk of physical or emotional harm are protected and those at lower risk, along with their families, are supported and strengthened through their community or neighbourhood networks. Families may be assigned to either child protection or family enhancement streams based upon assessment of risk and family willingness to engage with services to ameliorate difficulties or concerns identified during the assessment process. Second, strengthening links between local community based child and family services and better coordination of referral systems enables families to access a full range of services. Third, earlier permanency planning, developed in consultation with extended family, clinical specialists, and community partners, is emphasized to provide the opportunity for stable, permanent relationships for children in care. Finally, the implementation of processes and criteria to monitor outcomes, based on the national Child Welfare Indicator Matrix is a central component of ARM.

Introduction

In November 2001, the Alberta Government approved a set of significant policy changes collectively referred to as the Alberta Response Model. By early 2002, implementation began across the province.

The Alberta Response Model consists of several complex activities that address both the short- and long-term needs of the children, youth, and families who come into contact with the child welfare system. Its goal is to transform outcomes for children and youth by supporting and strengthening families. Its success depends upon community partners such as all levels of government, not-for-profit organizations, businesses, corporations, and voluntary community sectors playing a role in supporting children, youth, and families in their communities.

Transformational change of child welfare systems: The Alberta Response Model

In 2001, provincial and territorial ministers responsible for child welfare requested that Directors of Child Welfare from across Canada join together to examine the factors shaping child welfare systems and share expertise in order to find ways to resolve common issues, better serve children and youth and improve outcomes. The result was *New directions in child welfare,* a discussion paper (included in this publication) recommending a more customized approach to service delivery.

ARM adapts the New Directions approach to the particular resources and needs of the province. It builds on the successful practices introduced in the Alberta Children's Services redesign that promoted community based service delivery through Child and Family Services Authorities (CFSAs), early intervention supports, service integration, and Aboriginal involvement. Furthermore, it introduces transformational change in both service delivery and community engagement.

The implementation of ARM is based on the principle that protecting children, preventing maltreatment, and strengthening families form a service continuum. This important concept builds on the role of regional CFSAs and key community based partners such as Family and Community Support Services (FCSS) to support families along that service continuum.

FCSS is a longstanding partnership between the provincial government, municipalities, and Metis settlements. Under FCSS, communities design and deliver preventive social programs to enhance the quality of life for individuals and families in the community and to build capacity to prevent or deal with crisis situations should they arise. From the onset, FCSS has been involved in the development of ARM at the governance level and through regionally based partnerships and through the planning, development, and delivery of preventive social programs in communities across Alberta.

ARM is comprised of four interrelated core strategies and these strategies are implemented through the service delivery networks described above. The four strategies are:

1. Building on community or neighbourhood networks

In building community or neighbourhood networks, FCSS, CFSAs, and other partners strengthen the links between local, community based child and family support services by working with them more closely. Referral systems are better coordinated, so families can access the full range of services regardless of the "door" through which they entered. Other community or neighbourhood network partners reflect the needs, resources, and culture of the local community and the children and youth in those communities. These may include family violence prevention and addictions programs and services, fetal alcohol syndrome services, educators, health and mental health professionals, Aboriginal services, and a wide range of community based, privately funded organizations.

It is important to connect families to the types of lifelong supports found in communities that do not require open child welfare status to receive the help they need. However, there may be situations where the services needed by a family require the financial support of the CFSAs. In those cases, the differential response streaming process is unaffected by factors related to cost, with the focus on the appropriate service provision to reduce risk and promote child well-being.

2. Providing differential response

In the past, referrals to child welfare services received a standardized response that involved an initial screening, an assessment of the need for child protection, and an investigation if necessary. If the child was found to be safe, the case was closed. Canadian studies show approximately 70% of referrals are closed at intake or after the initial assessment (Trocmé et al., 2001). This statistic indicates that most families referred to child welfare do not need continued child protection.

While this one-size-fits-all approach ensured investigations were conducted in a consistent manner that would withstand legal and public scrutiny, it fell short of meeting the needs of the majority of referrals: families experiencing stress and in need of support services but not formal child protection. Differential response models address this gap in services, providing a mechanism for early identification of vulnerable children and families and mobilizing the necessary support services before a crisis occurs.

Differential response processes strive to be non-adversarial in nature and encourage CFSAs responsible for child welfare to work with the family and the community as partners in protecting children. A primary objective of this approach is to assist parents in performing their natural roles and fulfilling their responsibilities as caregivers for their children.

The initial screening and assessment process remains the same. However, under the differential response model, when a family is referred to the CFSA, the CFSA worker will identify the most appropriate stream during screening, using carefully designed criteria. The family may enter one of two streams:

The *child protection stream* is suitable for cases in which the child is at high risk of physical or emotional maltreatment and/or the family is unwilling or unable to voluntarily address their problems. The need for child protection services will be assessed and an investigation conducted, if necessary. The child and family will also be provided with the necessary supports and services to ensure child safety and promote child well-being.

The *family enhancement stream* is appropriate for cases in which the child is at lower risk but the family is vulnerable. If the family is willing, a comprehensive family assessment is conducted to identify the needs of the child and the strengths of the family, the extended family, and the community. Relevant community or neighbourhood network partners will then be asked to collaborate as members of a multidisciplinary team to develop an individualized plan connecting the family with community based services to help them meet their child's needs. A Family Enhancement worker will remain involved while a client accesses community based services. The Family Enhancement worker in addition to available community resources is also, through a reduced caseload, the direct provider of services to effect change. At the point the needs of the family have been met or can be met by the community services alone, the file will be closed. For the family enhancement approach to be successful, families must be willing to become actively involved in assessing their own needs and strengths and must be willing to work with other team members in planning and accessing needed services.

If the Family Enhancement worker believes the voluntary nature of the involvement has changed, or the risk level for the child(ren) is becoming high, the situation is referred back to screening. This not only ensures the family is receiving services in the correct stream, but allows the Family Enhancement worker to remain true to their role in the provision of less intrusive, voluntary service provision.

3. Increasing permanency planning

A central premise of differential response models is that the capacity of families to provide stable, nurturing environments for their children is strengthened with the support of community, neighbourhood and extended family networks. However, protective care will be required for some children and providing care remains an important role for government.

Among children and youth not reunited with their families, social, emotional, and academic development may be compromised by the instability that often characterizes foster care experiences. Earlier permanency planning for children in permanent government care provides the opportunity for stable and permanent relationships with parents or caregivers.

Within ARM, a permanency plan is developed shortly after case opening, with the specific goal of securing a stable placement for the child or helping to build a nurturing relationship with a dependable adult as quickly as possible, preferably within one year. To provide children and youth with the best opportunity for positive outcomes, permanency planning:

- Supports and plans family reunification, where possible
- Involves extended families earlier
- Establishes more specific standards for permanency planning
- Increased adoptions for children in permanent protective care (e.g., through the implementation of an adoption website)
- Supports children, youth, and families who are adjusting to a new family unit.

The extended family and relevant community or neighbourhood network partners are invited to participate in the development of the plan and to offer support, if able to do so. For Aboriginal children, the CFSA will seek the guidance and support of First Nations, Metis communities, and other Aboriginal groups. In addition, clinical specialists are consulted to ensure that decisions are well informed.

The range of options includes parental care, adoption, open adoption, care within the extended family (relative care), supported relative care, custom care for Aboriginal children, formalized long-term foster care, independent living, and in some cases, group care (living in a group home setting). The most suitable option depends upon the specific needs of the child or youth and strengths of the family, the extended family, and the community.

Whichever option is chosen, stability will be of utmost importance. If at all possible, children will be given the opportunity to establish or continue healthy, nurturing relationships with parents, relatives, and others who are significant in their life while awaiting a permanent placement. Visitations and other ways will be found to maintain these important ties.

4. Evaluating Outcomes

The success of any child welfare system comes down to one question: How well are the children doing? Greater utilization of community or neighbourhood networks, differential response, and earlier permanency planning is expected to result in better outcomes for vulnerable children, youth, and families.

In our 2003–2006 Ministry Business Plan, Alberta has committed to reporting on four of the 10 National Outcome Indicators as identified in Client Outcomes in Child Welfare: Phase II (Trocmé, Nutter, MacLaurin, & Fallon, 1999). These indicators are:

1. Recurrence of maltreatment
2. Serious injuries/deaths
3. Family moves
4. Grade level/graduation.

A minimum of four additional indicators will be added in the next business planning cycle.

Measuring outcomes with respect to child safety, child and family well-being, and the success of permanent placements will provide opportunities to evaluate ARM outcomes, monitor how services are delivered, and identify areas for improvement. Each CFSA is implementing processes and criteria to monitor outcomes, based on the national Child Welfare Indicator Matrix. This process of ongoing evaluation also involves developing strategies for exchanging information with community or neighbourhood network partners. Through the use of informed consents as well as aggregate data, the sharing of outcomes related information can be used to effectively plan for the continuous improvement of services for Alberta's children and families.

Summary

ARM retains as a fundamental objective providing protection to children at risk for future maltreatment. However, within this model, children identified as lower risk, whose families are willing to work at solving their own problems, are no longer left to manage with few supports. Instead, based upon an individualized plan that recognizes family strengths, needs, and resources, they are linked by the CFSA to a comprehensive system of community based supports through community and extended family networks. Outcomes will be formally reported on an annual basis, with the ability to access data over the course of the year for information and planning purposes. By defining the desired outcomes, measuring how well they are achieved on a case-by-case basis, and comparing the data over time, Alberta can objectively assess how successful ARM is in achieving the goal of transforming outcomes for Alberta's children, youth, and families.

USMA: Cherished ones, precious ones, the children
A First Nations approach to child, family, and community well-being

Debra Foxcroft and Cindy Blackstock

Abstract

This chapter examines emerging models of Aboriginal child welfare in British Columbia, particularly the development and implementation of a model of delegated authority in the USMA child welfare agency that serves the member bands of the Nuu-chah-nulth Tribal Council. In 1987, the USMA Nuu-chah-nulth Family and Child Services built upon provincial child welfare authority to develop child welfare programs that were based on Aboriginal values and traditions. Developing an Aboriginal system of child and family services that would be embraced as an integral part of the movement to strengthen families and communities required a set of community engagement processes to engage community participation and support. This chapter explores three essential features of this process including community education, community consultation, and the integration of holistic perspectives and concludes with a discussion of how Aboriginal self-government and empowerment require changes in the distribution of power and authority for determining child and family services legislation, policy, and practice.

Introduction

The British Columbia Ministry of Children and Family Development (2002) estimates that although Aboriginal peoples represent 5% of the provincial population, 35.8% of the children in care are Aboriginal. The over-representation of Aboriginal children and youth in care reflects the impacts of colonization and the imposition of culturally biased child welfare practices. The response to perceived difficulties within Aboriginal families historically favoured separation and placement over using or enhancing Aboriginal community support systems (Union of BC Indian Chiefs, 2002).

The residential school policy of the Government of Canada required First Nations parents to send their children between the ages of five and 15 years to schools operated by Christian churches. Upon arrival at the schools, children were separated by gender and forbidden from wearing traditional dress, speaking their language, and practicing their culture and spirituality. Contact with parents and extended family was limited. Malnutrition, overcrowding, and poor heating and ventilation were common and as a result, diseases such as smallpox and tuberculosis proliferated. Disease, abuse, and neglect resulted in child death rates ranging from 11% to 40% per annum (Royal Commission on Aboriginal Peoples, 1996). The Alberni residential school operated by the United Church was located in Nuu-chah-nulth territory. Students of the Alberni School reported serious abuse and neglect and in 1998, the Supreme Court of British Columbia confirmed that the United Church was vicariously liable for the abuse of the children in school. The last residential school in BC closed in 1984.

It was not until the mid 1950s that the Province of British Columbia began providing child welfare services on reserve. Operating with very limited understanding of the culture and context of First Nations peoples, provincial social workers removed large numbers of children from communities and placed them in non-Aboriginal foster homes. This large scale removal became known as "the sixties scoop" (Union of BC Indian Chiefs, 2002). To avoid the perpetuation of such practices, First Nations communities have been advocating for jurisdiction over the provision of their own child welfare services, as was recently done through the Nisga'a Treaty. Increasing numbers of First Nations are achieving this objective through the inclusion of child welfare authority in self government agreements. However many others, including the Nuu-chah-nulth, deliver services under the ambit of delegated provincial authority and federal funding. The delegated arrangement presents significant challenges as described by Durst (1996):

> …within the context of such agreements, a scenario can arise in which the "feds" hold the purse strings and the province has the legal hammer and the band is left to the dirty and impossible task of addressing major social problems with insufficient human and fiscal resources. The level of self-government in child welfare is currently capped at a co-management/delegated self-government, given the federal position that provincial legislation is the final authority. (p. 41)

This chapter explores how the first delegated Aboriginal child welfare agency in BC, USMA Family and Child Services, managed these issues and maintained its focus on child well-being within a Nuu-chah-nulth based community development framework.

Delegated model of Aboriginal child welfare in BC

There are only three treaties with First Nations in British Columbia: the Nisga'a Treaty, the Douglas Treaties, and Treaty 8. The rest of the province's First Nations are subject to treaty negotiations. To guide these negotiations, in 1991 the province adopted the BC Treaty Process—a six-step process involving the federal, provincial, and First Nations governments. Many First Nations, including the Nuu-chah-nulth Tribal Council (NTC), are including child welfare services in their treaty negotiations to eventually allow for affirmation of tribal laws. The treaty negotiation process is complicated and subject to changes in political agendas and progress has been slow.

For many years, the provincial and federal governments intentionally disrupted and disregarded First Nations systems of government, such as by banning of the Potlatch ceremony and instituting the Indian Act. There has recently been some effort by both levels of government to support First Nations in establishing "culturally appropriate" child welfare services, although British Columbia continues to require First Nations child and family service agencies to adhere to provincial child welfare legislation and regulations. Typically, the province delegates child welfare authority through a tripartite delegation agreement with the First Nation, while the federal Department of Indian Affairs and Northern Development (DIAND) funds the agency according to a funding formula known as Directive 20-1. A review of this directive conducted in 2000 by DIAND and the Assembly of First Nations (AFN) confirmed many NTC concerns regarding the delegated model. These include the inadequate emphasis on prevention and community development within the funding formula and a lack of connection between funding and policy. The review recommended that future funding policies support tribal child welfare laws (McDonald & Ladd, 2000).

BC child welfare legislation is premised on the Euro-western concept of individual rights, in contrast to First Nations' communal traditions. Many community members question why First Nations are obliged to use child welfare legislation and practices that have had proven so ineffective and detrimental. The concept of child removal has no tradition in First Nations teachings; when parents were unable to care for their children, they were placed with other community members without severing the parental relationship. The history of forcibly removing children from First Nations communities for placement in residential schools and for adoption in non-Aboriginal communities led the USMA Family and Child Services to develop alternative child welfare practices, acknowledging and affirming community capacity to care for children instead of taking them away. This required working with Nuu-chah-nulth leadership, community members, and agencies throughout the agency's development and operation.

USMA Family and Child Services

In 1970, the NTC completed a study of the child and family services provided to them by the provincial government. Emerging from this study, the NTC established in 1985 a tribal-based delegated child and family service agency. The agency (given the name USMA meaning "cherished ones, precious ones" by the Nuu-chah-nulth Elders) began providing child welfare services in 1988. Over the next 16 years, USMA program administration and staff worked with community members to develop an alternative model of child and family services that embodied Aboriginal values and traditions while continuing to meet provincial statutory requirements. Within the holistic approach the best interests of the child includes the provision of a full range of culturally appropriate services that promote the health and well-being of children within the context of supported relationships with their families, communities and culture.

Protecting and promoting the well-being of Aboriginal children requires more than the implementation of Euro-western child welfare services by Aboriginal people for Aboriginal people. It requires a constructive decolonization of child welfare pedagogy and practice and the development of new approaches that affirm Aboriginal ways of knowing and being. It also calls for an acknowledgement of community members' mistrust of child welfare services based on inappropriate child welfare practice and the residential school systems. Developing a system of child and family services that would be embraced as an integral part of the movement to strengthen families and communities required a set of processes to engage the community and engender support among its members.

In 1993, following an organizational review conducted by USMA staff, child and family services were integrated with health, education, counselling, infant development, and social services for a more holistic and integrated system of care. Three essential features marked USMA's evolution toward more culturally based practice: community education, community consultation, and the integration of holistic ways of knowing and being into child welfare.

Community education

From the beginning, USMA administrators knew that in order to optimize program effectiveness and to engage the community in affirming and promoting the well-being of children, the community had to be involved in the development of the new services. USMA reached out to the Nuu-chah-nulth community and tribal council leadership to raise awareness about child maltreatment and engage them in community based education programs to identify and respond to child maltreatment. Engagement required frank and open conversations about how the provincial child welfare system had negatively affected Nuu-chah-nulth children and their families. These conversations inspired the development of community accountability mechanisms for the agency in order to ensure child well-being within a culturally based community development context. Changing perceptions and attitudes and building trust at the community level has been a gradual process aided by community education and demonstration of respectful and effective practice by the USMA agency. This has required an ongoing commitment to open dialogue and to increasing community awareness and engagement through newsletters, newspapers, videos, meetings, and annual events. The objectives of these programs have been to increase the community's understanding of the design, structure, and practice of child welfare agencies and to develop ways for community members to contribute to child well-being.

A key step in this process was the development of a community declaration against family violence. Nuu-chah-nulth women advocated for, and received, community support for a zero tolerance policy towards family violence within Nuu-chah-nulth tribal communities.

Consultation

Extensive, ongoing consultation and collaboration with community groups including Nuu-chah-nulth Elders, children, and parents, have been essential to identify community needs and guide agency responses to meet those needs. Significant attention was paid to the development and maintenance of healthy and knowledgeable advisory committees and staff. Whenever possible, the agency affirmed the community's capacity to care for their children by hiring qualified Nuu-chah-nulth staff and including community members on advisory committees. This capacity building, coupled with the agency commitment to support professional and organizational learning, facilitated communication and provided children and youth with positive role models. Roles and responsibilities were clarified through protocol agreements acknowledging skills and responsibilities and providing mechanisms for the coordination of roles.

Community consultation also played a key role in the recruitment and maintenance of out-of-home placements within the Nuu-chah-nulth Nation to ensure that when removals are required, children remain in the community—connected to their culture and family. USMA hosts regular honouring ceremonies to acknowledge the important role that caregivers play in ensuring the welfare of Nuu-chah-nulth children and youth.

Consultation was also extended beyond the community level to include other First Nations who were developing or operating their own child and family service agencies. This network of First Nations agencies was eventually formalized through terms of reference and regular meetings. Gaining access to culturally based professional development services for social workers was a key concern for all agencies and resulted in the development of a provincial non-profit organization, the Caring for First Nations Children Society, which developed and delivered an eight-week training program for social workers employed by Aboriginal child welfare agencies. This organization, coupled with USMA's affiliations with the Native Indian Child Welfare Association in the United States and the First Nations Summit Child Welfare Committee in British Columbia, provided the agency with forums for collective learning and support.

The holistic approach

The development of child and family services was guided by the overarching principle that child welfare must be integrated within systems of service that strengthen Aboriginal families. There were two essential features of service delivery in these communities. As stated in its mission statement, USMA provides protective services to families living on Nuu-chah-nulth reserves by investigating reports of child abuse and neglect and ensuring the safety and support of children who are victims of abuse and neglect. Second, the welfare of children is protected while simultaneously investing in programs that redress systemic risk factors arising from colonization. Multidimensional and multigenerational service responses are required to deal with the consequences of colonial policies that had a negative impact on our communities. USMA also supports community development programs, such as suicide prevention and hosting workshops to redress the impacts of residential schools. All available resources are activated both within and, when appropriate, outside of the community. Thus, the welfare of children is conceptualized more broadly, within the context of healthy families and communities.

Incorporating genealogy workers and teachings of Elders facilitated the development of a system that instilled pride and affirmed the values and traditions of Aboriginal communities. Genealogy workers help children understand their family history, which strengthens the child's sense of identity and has the additional benefit of identifying family members who could be called upon to provide care and support for the child and his or her family.

Contemporary challenges and opportunities

As the USMA agency continues to work with the community in order to optimize services provided under the delegated model, the agency is continuing negotiations with the provincial Ministry of Children and Family Development to extend the USMA mandate off reserve. USMA has always felt a responsibility to Nuu-chah-nulth children regardless of their place of residency. The complicating factor has been that extending the mandate off reserve meant getting the financial and statutory support of the province because the federal government does not fund child welfare services for off-reserve residents. In 1999, the province recognized "that the Nuu-chah-nulth have an inherent responsibility for their children, wherever they may live in British Columbia" (British Columbia Ministry for Children and Families, 1999). Despite this recognition, USMA has yet to receive the provincial support needed to extend its mandate to provide child welfare services to Nuu-chah-nulth children and youth living off reserve. Negotiations continue to change the delegated arrangement so that Nuu-chah-nulth members residing anywhere in British Columbia can receive USMA services.

Another challenge for the agency will be to effectively bridge the transition to a self government model of child welfare once a treaty is signed. Community development and engagement will again be critical when the agency shifts from a joint community and provincial accountability framework to one where accountability rests solely with the community.

Other challenges include continued investment in community development to address the systemic drivers of child maltreatment in Nuu-chah-nulth communities, such as substance abuse, poverty, social exclusion, and lack of meaningful recognition of personal and collective rights. Despite these challenges, the Nuu-chah-nulth are committed to moving forward in a way that honours the knowledge of their ancestors. Sustainable positive change is rooted in a community approach to child welfare and reflects the best traditions of Nuu-chah-nulth teachings, which celebrate the ability of all community members to contribute to the care of children.

The inclusive approach of the Outaouais Centres jeunesse*

Gilles Clavel, Luc Cadieux, and Catherine Roy

Abstract

Quebec's legislation and regulations define child welfare and child protection as collective community responsibilities. The Centres jeunesse, which are the provincial agencies mandated to identify children at risk and ensure their protection, seek the support of community organizations to assist and support them in fulfilling their responsibilities. However, it is difficult to achieve the accessibility, continuity, and consistency of social services for children and families due to a fragmented system. This chapter details the efforts to overcome barriers to services by the Outaouais Centres jeunesse in western Quebec, through the adoption of an inclusive approach. This approach is family-focused and has three guiding principles for interventions. Efforts must be made to understand the positive and negative aspects of an individual child's situation, mobilize all available and necessary community resources, and involve parents and/or other caregivers in the development of the child's individualized service plan. This chapter also outlines collaborative intervention programs, inspired by the inclusive approach.

Child welfare in Quebec: Past and present

Since Quebec's Youth Protection Act (YPA) was introduced in 1979, a number of reviews have been conducted to analyze the accessibility, continuity, and consistency of services, the application of protective measures, and the degree of collaboration among service providers.[1] The various reviews resulted in a variety of recommendations, but all agreed on the need for a collective effort

---

* This article was translated from French by Eve Krakow.

1 Reports most frequently cited include that of the Commission d'enquête sur le service de santé et des services sociaux (Rochon, 1988); *Un Québec fou de ses enfants* (Rapport Bouchard, 1991); *La protection sur mesure, un projet collectif* (Rapport Harvey, 1991); *Les jeunes contrevenants, au nom...et au-delà de la Loi* (Rapport Jasmin, 1995); *Pour une stratégie de soutien du développement des enfants et des jeunes, agissons complices* (Rapport Cliché, 1998); and the report of the Commission d'étude sur les services de santé et les services sociaux (Rapport Clair, 2000).

to provide children and families with services tailored to their needs. This recommendation is echoed in the provincial regulations, contained in the "Youth Protection Reference Manual" or *Manuel de référence sur la protection de la jeunesse* (Groupe de travail, 1998). The manual states that the Director of Youth Protection must use the services and resources available in the community for children whose security or development is in danger.

Moreover, child welfare is considered a collective responsibility. Services provided under the Youth Protection Act must recognize the individual as an active member of the community. At the same time, the community must be perceived as a group of individuals who share resources and who actively seek solutions to the problems affecting them, individually or collectively. There are many objectives of the child protection mission entrusted to the Centres jeunesse du Quebec which provide child welfare services in the province. These objectives include identifying children at risk, ensuring their protection, preventing their placement in out-of-home care, and strengthening the family. When placement is necessary, the child should be provided with an alternate living environment that is as stable and as permanent as possible. The support of community organizations is essential to achieving these objectives.

However, accessibility, continuity, and consistency of services are sometimes difficult to achieve, given the fragmentation of the current social services system. In particular, "specialized" front-line services are frequently unavailable, especially when a child is placed in out-of-home care. The organization delivering the specialized services (i.e., the Centre de jeunesse) is expected to meet all the needs of the child and his or her family. This is a very heavy responsibility for an organization whose services are often centralized and defined by very specific institutional and legal mandates.

The inclusive approach in the Outaouais

In an effort to make child protection a truly collective responsibility, the Centres jeunesse in the Outaouais region of Quebec have developed an action plan whose main objective is increasing partnerships with other institutional and community organizations in the region. Collaboration is therefore the key feature of the operating philosophy: the inclusive approach.

The family is at the core of the inclusive approach. The underlying assumptions are the active participation of the family involved, capitalizing on the competencies of all family members, and recognizing that the parents are primarily responsible for the protection of their children. By adopting an inclusive approach, the Outaouais Centres jeunesse have chosen to consider the children, youth, and parents receiving services as active contributors to their own development with resources essential to their growth. More specifically, the inclusive approach has the following fundamental goal:

> To enable any child or adolescent to maintain and develop ties to his/her family and community and to take all necessary steps to foster collaboration with the resources in this community in order to support this child or youth and his/her family, within the context of an intervention plan or service. [translation][2]

Under the inclusive approach, a child protection intervention is meaningful only if it is carried out in close collaboration with community partners. In fact, with the inclusive approach, children who experience difficulties are seen as needing more support from their environment and therefore being entitled to greater access to services. In other words, the child welfare intervention is conducted according to its own norms and standards but also with the primary objective of being carried out in the environment within the child and parents' environment.

Mandated child welfare interventions are governed by three guiding principles. First, efforts are made to understand the individual circumstances of a child reported to be in need of protection, both in terms of the positive and negative aspects of the child's situation. Second, a special effort is then made to mobilize all of the community, social, and medical services available in the child's neighbourhood. In this respect, responsibility for child protection is shared by all partners within the continuum of available services to the child or his or her family. All partners must share common values in terms of respecting the rights and interests of children, preserving families, and strengthening communities. Finally, an individualized service plan is a key intervention tool and its development is an opportunity for the partners to work in collaboration with the child, the parents or substitute caregivers, and the foster parents, if applicable.

In practical terms, the Outaouais Centres jeunesse action plan contains various strategies, all of which aim to provide better services to families with children whose safety or development is at risk. For example, despite the highest rate of reported cases in Quebec, only 35% to 40% of cases reported to the Outaouais Director of Youth Protection are found to

---

[2] From the 1999-2002 plan of the Outaouais Centres jeunesse, entitled "Un leadership puissant au service de la jeunesse," and approved by the board of directors on September 22, 1999.

require an investigation, compared to a provincial average of 45%. Of all the cases investigated, nearly two-thirds do not require protective measures, although some type of social or medical service may be recommended for the child or family. Previously, there was no clear agreement about responsibility for service provision in circumstances that did not require placing a child in out-of-home care but which still pose a threat to the child's security or development. Through partnership agreements with the Outaouais Centres jeunesse and the region's Centres locaux de service communautaire (or "local community service centres," which are provincial agencies providing preventive and curative health and social services), accessibility and continuity of services are now ensured for all children and families who need them.

Also as part of the action plan, the Outaouais Centres jeunesse set up a "site verification" program involving short-term and rapid intervention in a child's living situation as soon as the case is reported. This permits the diffusion of some situations and can reduce the total duration of interventions. Moreover, when state intervention is not required, the site verification can be used to direct the child and family to resources outside the child welfare system. In more than 80% of site verification cases, children and families have access to life-enhancing services more quickly than with a "traditional" service response.

Finally, other mechanisms, such as service provision meetings and collaboration protocols with other professions ensure better coordination of activities by various disciplines. The resulting collaboration fosters complementary service provision rather than duplication.

Implications of the inclusive approach

While it is essential to develop effective links among child protection and other sectors serving children and families, the main challenge remains the development and accessibility of services that meet the needs of children and youth who are reported to the Director of Youth Protection, whether they are protective or other types of services. Successful interventions from the inclusive approach adhere to a certain number of principles. First, workers are encouraged to think outside the institutional perspective to focus on the needs of the child and the family instead. This is a sizeable challenge for professionals accustomed to focusing on one particular aspect (i.e., ending a situation that endangers the child's security) within the framework of a specific mandate. Secondly, the channels of communication between managers and child welfare workers must be rethought to avoid top-down exchanges, in which managers and supervisors issue directives to be implemented by front-line workers. Communication should be two-way and cut across the hierarchy. In addition, workers from other organizations called upon to work with child welfare to assist a child or family must also develop mechanisms for clear, respectful, and efficient dialogue. Finally, a sense of responsibility, involvement, and commitment by workers is crucial to successful inclusive-approach interventions. To this end, continuous training and opportunities to develop new competencies help maintain workers' motivation and recognize their work with children and families.

Examples of programs

Four examples of intervention programs, all inspired by the inclusive approach, are presented in Table 1. These programs have been developed at the Outaouais Centres jeunesse and illustrate how child protection can be carried out in collaboration with partners from other fields. Although three of the four projects have not yet been evaluated, all their experiences nonetheless demonstrate how certain factors can facilitate or hinder the implementation and application of an inclusive approach. For example, in the project called "Parcours vers l'adaptation," the lack of continuity in services proved to be a major obstacle. The workers and partners involved in this program confirmed the importance of bridging child welfare and adult services for youth nearing the age of majority. At times, the lack of connection between child and adult services slowed or limited a young person's successful transition to adulthood. One can assume that this represents a barrier to successful interventions for young people. In the "Familles en envol" project, workers at the youth centres, the CLSCs, and community organizations all embraced the same concept of protection. This common vision not only helped the project run smoothly, but contributed to mutual respect for various partners' strengths and weaknesses. This was no doubt a factor in the intervention's success.

Evaluation and indicators of success

As noted in Table 1, the programs implemented under the inclusive approach have not yet been evaluated. However, some of the preliminary observations are quite promising. Results of an evaluation study of the implementation of agreements between CLSCs and youth centres have ranked the Outaouais region an easy first (Larivière et al., 2000). The Outaouais distinguishes itself from other regions in Quebec on several fronts. It has the largest number of formal mechanisms for collaboration and a facility for creating and maintaining relationships with partner organizations. The Outaouais region also has the largest number of initiatives promoting health and well-being, in proportion to existing resources. There is no doubt, however, that monitoring and evaluating the procedures and results of these interventions is essential. The Outaouais Centres jeunesse recognize this important need and are working to integrate a systemic mechanism to evaluate the interventions resulting from the inclusive approach.

Conclusion

The complexity of family situations and the reluctance of many families to become involved in an intervention procedure can result in the children and the parents being excluded from the decision-making process when preventive or protective measures are required. The inclusive approach considers that the child's immediate living environment, as well as the people who are part of that environment, are the primary agents of the child's development and indispensable resources to the child's growth. Thus, the protection intervention is meaningful only in so far as it is carried out in direct cooperation with the partners and stakeholders, which requires an intense collaborative effort. The experience of the Outaouais Centres jeunesse suggests that this way of framing child protection can be very promising. While it may not be sufficient on its own, the inclusive approach increases the likelihood that children and families at risk will have access to quality services adapted to their needs.

Table 1. Projects underway and inspired by the inclusive approach of the Outaouais Centres jeunesse

Project	Main	Partners objective	Evaluation	Success indicators
Les jeunes et la nuit	Prevent night-time vandalism by youth	- City of Maniwaki - Sécurité du Québec - CLSC Vallée de la Gatineau - Maison des jeunes Mani-Jeunes - First Nations community of Kitigan Zabi	Not yet evaluated	Decrease in neighbourhood delinquency rate
Moi je m'organise	Employment skills for young people	- Municipalities - Centre d'emploi Québec - Commission scolaire des Draveurs - Cascade (private company)	Not yet evaluated	Number of young people integrated into the job market

Table 1. Projects underway *(continued)*

Project	Main objective	Partners	Evaluation	Success indicators
Familles en envol	Improve the quality of life and parent/child relations in families dealing with neglect, by increasing community involvement	- Solidarité Gatineau-Ouest (community organization) - CLSC de Gatineau	In progress	Fewer reports of neglect Number of files closed and opened under the LSSSS (Act Respecting Health Services and Social Services)
Parcours vers l'adaptation	Accompany young people in their transitions to adulthood	- Vallée Jeunesse (community organization) - University of Ottawa (criminology interns) - Université du Québec en Outaouais (psycho-education interns) - Commission scolaire de Gatineau - Emploi-Québec	Not yet evaluated	Number of young people referred to adult services

Integrating children's services: A perspective from England

Helen Jones, Ellen Chant, and Harriet Ward

Abstract

Growing numbers of children in the United Kingdom are experiencing difficulties which affect their well-being and achievement, whether in relation to education, health, or quality of care. It is beyond the capacity of child welfare agencies to be solely responsible for meeting these levels of need in their communities. Cross-government policy for children is therefore focused increasingly on multi-agency early intervention for children and their families. Effective early intervention strategies require close, collaborative working between universal, targeted and specialist services to ensure that appropriate and timely responses are provided.

This chapter explores the challenges to the effectiveness of prevention posed by the fragmentation of policy and services for children and their families at central and local government levels. It also describes how a systems approach to child welfare and an outcomes framework which applies to all children and is based on their developmental needs are key to the development of multi-agency collaboration and service delivery. These and other elements which are required to support integrated working are illustrated and explored through a detailed case study of the development of a common methodology for assessing need used in one locality, North Lincolnshire, by all agencies working with children and families.

Introduction

In England, policy making is a highly centralized function. Such a system offers both opportunities and challenges which must be acknowledged in order to ensure effective practice. A major opportunity lies in the possibility of local agencies using common frameworks to ensure that children and their families receive a consistent response. The challenge is to ensure that the framework offers sufficient space for adaptation to local needs and circumstances. This balance is explored within the context of the development of the North Lincolnshire model of needs assessment.

The causes and effects of fragmentation

In England, several government departments are responsible for legislation and policy for children. Each sets practice guidelines and has its own targets and performance monitoring system. Even more significantly, each ministry has responsibility for a particular aspect of children's lives—education, health, youth justice, child welfare including protection—and has developed assessment tools to identify needs in relation to their particular interest. A simplified diagram at Figure 1 illustrates the issue.

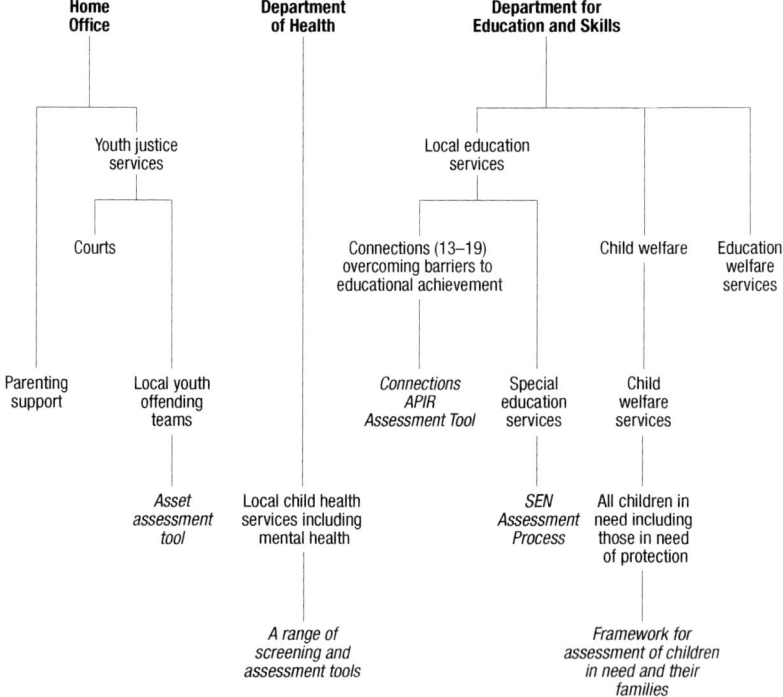

Figure 1. Government departments and local service delivery

Thus the Home Office, responsible for youth justice, has supported the development of the Asset assessment tool to identify young people's risks of further offending; the Department of Health, responsible for child welfare services until June 2003, requires practitioners to use the Framework for the Assessment of Children in Need to explore the relationship between parental capacity, family and environmental factors, and children's developmental progress; local health authorities employ a further range of screening and assessment tools to identify health needs; the Department for Education and Skills has developed further materials to assess children's educational progress and their special educational needs.

The effects of such fragmentation are significant, particularly from the perspective of service users, who frequently have to recite the same story to different agencies only to end up feeling alienated from all. Indeed such multiple assessments may lead to no service at all and different agencies have different thresholds for services. Rivalry over which is the key agency and lack of trust in the professional skills of others is common. Cases which arouse any anxiety are always handed to child welfare services, resulting in overwhelming numbers of referrals. A vicious circle may develop in child welfare where, in response to high referral rates, threshold criteria are raised so that child protection becomes the level at which services can be accessed. Concerns about a child and family will then be expressed by other agencies as child protection concerns in order to ensure a response. Overall it becomes impossible to deliver a service which looks at the needs of the whole child and the family.

Fragmentation will not be overcome without activity at both local and national levels. At both levels, the development of a holistic understanding of the needs of children and their families and a systemic approach to multi-agency working are required. A systemic approach is key as children may be part of several different systems at the same time, receiving a universal service through education, while the family receives a targeted service such as a home visiting program, and the child receives a specialist service such as play therapy. A systemic approach also provides a way of understanding how changes in the way one agency delivers services will affect other agencies providing services to children and their families. Underpinning this will be the establishment of a clear vision across services of the joint aims, the contribution of each service, and an understanding that success will be measured within a common outcomes framework.

The developmental approach

The development of a national outcomes framework has been fundamental to service development in England. The assessment model used in all child welfare agencies uses a framework which describes children's needs and the capacity of parents to meet those needs within the context of wider family and environmental factors. The framework is described at Figure 2. The development of this framework has been made possible by the positive relationships between research, policy, and practice to ensure both an evidence based approach to policy making and the engagement of practitioners.

Figure 2. Assessment framework

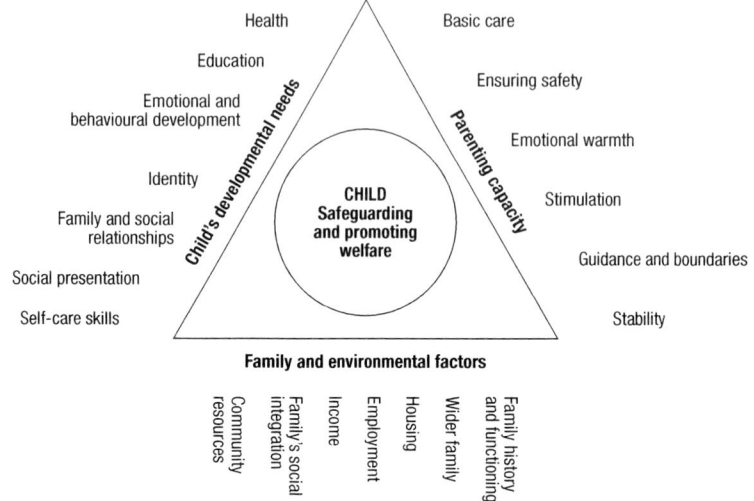

In 1991, Hardiker, Exton, & Barker identified the key issue for child welfare as changing the focus from asking if a child has been abused to asking about the child's need for services, including protection.

At the same time, the Looking After Children Project (Parker, Ward, Jackson, Aldgate, & Wedge, 1991) was identifying how the progress of children in care should be assessed across a spectrum of seven developmental dimensions: health, education, emotional and behavioural development, identity, family and social relationships, social presentation, and self-care skills. These would eventually be at the heart of the new assessment framework for all children in need and their families and would underpin the objectives set by the government for child welfare services. These objectives set actions and targets in important areas of attachment, health, education, and others which affect children's life chances.

Moves towards effective integration at the national level

While relevant government departments with responsibilities for children still produce separate legislation, significant progress has been made in the achievement of an underpinning vision and outcomes framework which will be common to all. This draft national strategy identifies six key areas for monitoring outcomes for all children: health and well-being, achievement and enjoyment, participation and citizenship, protection, responsibility, and inclusion (Children and Young People's Unit, 2001). Activity is also underway to harmonize assessments within a common framework using a common language to describe children's needs and reducing unnecessary duplication. This is likely to be based around the domains and dimensions of the assessment framework (United Kingdom Department of Health, Department of Education and Employment, and Home Office, 2000). Importantly such initiatives require some commonality in the information requirements of the assessments and data sharing capacity. The Looking After Children system and the Framework for the Assessment of Children in Need and their Families have now been combined to create the Integrated Children System (ICS) (United Kingdom Department of Health, 2003a) to provide a unified framework for assessment, planning, intervention, and review for all children and their families from first contact with child welfare. This provides a set of data requirements for child welfare, derived from individual children's records together with exemplar records for use by practitioners. As well as providing common terminology and a basis for identifying children's progress, the Integrated Children's System generates core information about children in need and their families and an opportunity for local agencies to improve multi-agency working, share information, and facilitate referrals between agencies.

The ICS is now being piloted on a multi-agency basis in four English child welfare agencies (United Kingdom Department of Health, 2003). Most recently, responsibility for children's social care policy was transferred from the Department of Health to the Department for Education and Skills in June 2003. This offers the opportunity for a greater alignment of children's policy across education, early years services, and social care but has the potential to increase the divide with children's health policy.

Integration of services at local level

So far, this chapter has described the necessary elements for effective integration of child welfare services in relation to initiatives and activity at the central government level. In the following discussion, the issues outlined above will be explored through a case study of the North Lincolnshire Approach to the Assessment of Children in Need, a multi-agency approach to the assessment of children introduced in one child welfare agency that anticipated national developments. We outline the context in which change at the local level was taking place together with the core elements and processes required to develop a "whole systems" approach and describe some of the key findings.

Before a common methodology for the assessment of need (the common assessment) is examined in detail, it is necessary to describe the historical context that instigated and shaped its formulation and development.

In 1996, North Lincolnshire was created as a new unitary authority with new management and political direction. This provided an ideal opportunity for the authority to evaluate the child welfare services it delivered from the point of referral through to resource availability and service provision. Within this evaluation the quality of multi-agency relationships and working arrangements were also examined.

The evaluation demonstrated that the services being provided to children and families and the effectiveness of the interagency working arrangements, while essentially protecting those children most at risk, were not addressing the needs of children who were not requiring protection. At this time, responses to child concern referrals were still framed by asking, "Has this child been abused?" There were several consequences of delivering services in this way. One was that the focus on abuse meant that referrals which did not indicate that a child required protection would be unsuccessful in gaining a social work response; referring agencies began to perceive that "if it was not child protection, then it did not exist."

The result was that all child concern referrals were framed in child protection terms in order to ensure that they resulted in action (United Kingdom Department of Health, 1995).

In practice, once the initial investigation had taken place, those referrals where abuse was unsubstantiated received little or no support services. A study sample of 199 child protection referrals made to North Lincolnshire Social Services in 1996 demonstrated that only 32 (16%) received a home based service and nine children (5%) were placed away from parents (see Figure 3). Moreover, when these cases were later reviewed, most had been re-referred into the system at a later date, often at the point of family breakdown or crisis (Thorpe, 1997).

Figure 3. Child protection referral outcomes—North Lincolnshire Council Social Services Directorate 1996

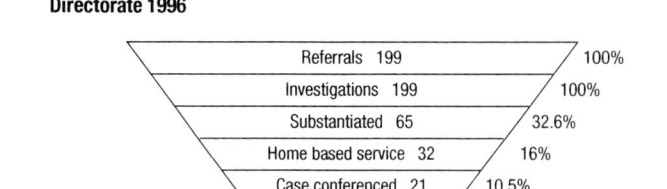

Understandably, families were highly mistrustful of, and alienated from, the child welfare service, describing a system that was largely intrusive, overly critical and unsupportive of them. They also felt that professionals approached the process looking for parental failure without acknowledging their strengths and achievements. Furthermore, the written assessment often bore little resemblance to the visit that had taken place. Parents also stated that they would be required to repeat their whole story for each professional who visited, resulting in delays in service provision.

Reviews of case files and consultation with other agencies and families identified that a further problem was the number of repeated assessments that took place before services were delivered. As professionals became accustomed to framing all referrals in child protection terms in order to ensure a response, so the social workers became mistrustful of other professionals' assessment and decision-making skills and would therefore repeat any previous assessments undertaken. This duplication then strengthened the culture in which each professional group would work to a different threshold of concern, so perpetuating the consequences of fragmentation in interagency working. The number of children placed on the child protection register and the number of children entering care were high and continued to rise as the system was deluged with over 65 referrals per week.

It became apparent that in order to reshape the child welfare service, the focus needed to be broadened to cover the question posed by Hardiker et al., (1991), and quoted at the beginning of this paper: "What are the needs of the child (including child protection), which cannot be met without the provision of services?" Such a shift would address the perception of referrers that services were only directed towards those children considered to be in need of protection and at the same time would re-balance the negative view of the child welfare service held by families.

A whole system approach

Clearly change needed to take place at more than one level to be effective. A six-point whole system approach to assessment and service delivery was therefore developed. This included:

1) A detailed population needs assessment, designed to give a broad view of the probable numbers of children in need within the area and their location.

2) A common assessment approach for all children in need of services,

which would be used by all professionals for children who require a referral into the child welfare system.

3) The introduction of a referral category of "child concern" to facilitate a more flexible response to referrals.

4) Consistent and clear analysis of needs assessment before the provision of further services under the legislative definitions of "child in need" (Section 17) and "child protection" (Section 47), with an emphasis on partnership working.

5) Consistent allocation of resources, dependent upon need.

6) Detailed planning and delivery of service requirements, dependent upon need.

Developing common standards for identifying children in need

The term "child in need" derives from the Children Act 1989, which seeks to identify the population of children in need of child welfare services. The Children Act 1989 (S17(10)) defines a child in need if:

(a) He is unlikely to achieve or maintain, or have the opportunity of achieving or maintaining, a reasonable standard of health or development without the provision for him of a service.
(b) His health or development is likely to be significantly impaired, or further impaired, without the provision for him of a service.
(c) He is disabled.

In order to improve services for children in need and their families, each agency and individual professional has been required to recognize and accept responsibility in identifying and responding appropriately to need. The point at which a professional raises concerns or identifies needs and the basis on which a decision is made to refer the child to the child welfare service play a fundamental part in determining whether the child and family receive a service and what the nature of that service will be.

Each agency had developed its own criteria and methodology for the assessment of need, and this had resulted in inconsistencies in the thresholds for intervention and service delivery. It was clear that if a consistent response to need was a key factor in the effective access and delivery of children's services, a common methodology for the identification of need, which was acceptable to and utilized by all agencies, was required.

Supported by a small research grant from the Department of Health, North Lincolnshire Child Welfare Service worked with Home Start (a local voluntary family visiting service) and Loughborough University to develop and pilot a common methodology for assessment, based on the developmental approach of the Looking After Children materials (United Kingdom Department of Health, 1991; see also Ward & Peel, 2002).

Following a consultation process with professionals at all levels and from different backgrounds to establish the training and key texts central to their practice, and a subsequent literature review (Peel & Ward, 1997), an extensive list of indicators of need were developed. These covered the seven dimensions of child development in the Looking After Children materials and included parenting and environmental factors, in line with the Framework for the Assessment of Children in Need and their Families (United Kingdom Department of Health, Department for Education and Employment, and Home Office, 2000).

The researchers then set up a number of focus groups whose task was to rank the indicators of need into areas of mild, moderate, or serious concern. Participants were advised that moderate concerns should correspond to the Children Act 1989, Section 17(10)(a) and serious concerns to Section 17 (10) (b) (see Figure 4). The focus groups were attended by over 250 professionals including health care workers, education workers, police officers, voluntary sector workers, and social workers; 46 parents, 14 of whom had previously had contact with the child welfare service were also included.

The three levels of concern should elicit responses commensurate with Hardiker et al.'s levels of intervention (2002). Thus, mild concerns would identify needs that will not in isolation require the provision of a child welfare service but may be met by universal services from health, education, or the voluntary sector. Moderate concerns would show that services are required possibly from a range of agencies within a specific time scale. Serious concerns would be likely to require an immediate response from a range of agencies and referral to the child welfare service would be necessary.

Despite substantial differences in professional backgrounds or experience of parenting, the indicators were ranked remarkably similarly, demonstrating that while professionals perceived that the thresholds for concern between different agencies were disparate, there was in reality a consensus which had previously gone unrecognised.

The identification of a hidden consensus between professionals and families concerning the standards to be employed in assessing whether and to what extent families require additional support facilitated the development of inter-professional trust in each other's judgement. Once professionals were able to subscribe to an agreed upon common standard, the mistrust which had led to repeated and duplicated assessments of need was minimized.

The common assessment

The common assessment tool provides the professional with a structured approach in assessing the needs of children and families. The assessments are age-banded in common with the Looking After Children materials to reflect the developmental needs of children and each individual child has a separate assessment completed. Wherever possible, the assessment is completed in the family home in partnership with the parents and, where appropriate, the child. Incorporating examples of the indicators at their locally agreed level allows professionals to make clear, evidence ased decisions about the observed needs of children and families in their area, to ascertain whether their needs are mild, moderate or serious, and to make referrals to agencies other than child welfare where appropriate.

Common assessment: A walk through the system

At the point at which any worker, irrespective of their profession, identifies a concern about a child, or a need is observed that does not constitute a child protection referral and the family is not currently working with the child welfare service, consent is obtained from the family (and child where age appropriate) to commence a common assessment. Families usually work with a range of services at any one time, from universal health and education services to targeted and specialist services; the worker initiating the assessment therefore ensures that where other services are working with the child and family, liaison takes place. Where appropriate, the assessment can be undertaken jointly between agencies, thus providing an opportunity for information sharing and the removal of the results of service fragmentation, as well as demonstrating to the family that agencies are working together to meet their needs. This also ensures that the consistency in thresholds of need between different professionals can be maintained. If the assessment identifies that a number of agencies are required to respond to the identified need, a multi-agency child in need meeting can be called to develop a coordinated plan of care and services. The multi-agency meeting is then recalled to ensure that the interventions are meeting the identified needs and ensuring that the child has not subsequently become in need of protection.

Figure 4. Procedures—Common assessment and the Child in Care meeting

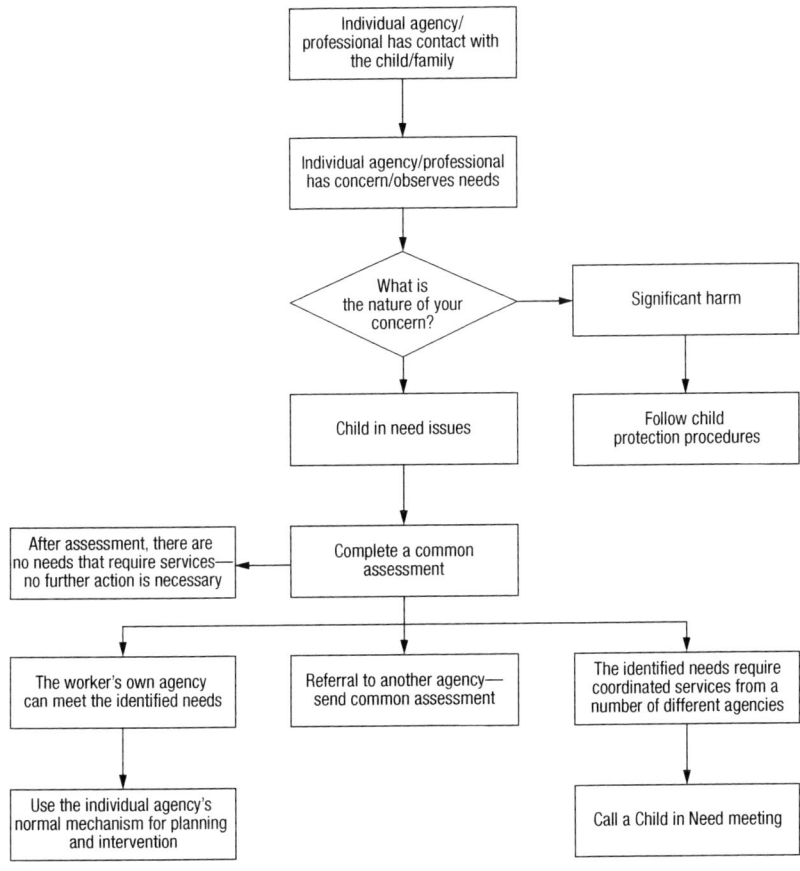

Flexibility within a common approach

It was recognized that if a common assessment methodology was to be successful and be able to cut across the range of different agencies working with children and families, a degree of flexibility would need to be created to ensure that all involved felt able to contribute to the process. This proved particularly fundamental to engaging groups of professionals who did not view the assessment of children's needs as their core business or who did not work with families in their own homes.

Two such professional groups who required a degree of flexibility of approach for differing reasons were teaching staff and police officers. While teaching staff felt able to adopt the principles around an interagency assessment process, many felt unable to accept that they would need to undertake a home visit to complete the task. It was important to ensure that the issue of the home visiting did not become a barrier to teaching staff, who are often best placed to identify and assess the needs of their pupils. A solution to this situation was found within the interagency working arrangements. Teaching staff were able to work jointly with allied education and health colleagues who undertake home visiting as part of their every day role. While the teacher now remains the main assessor, responsible for instigating the assessment and the engagement of the family, the assessment process can be commenced within the school environment, with a subsequent home visit to assess the physical environment being undertaken by a supporting colleague. This also allows the family the opportunity to explore their issues and concerns in their own environment. By affording the school this degree of flexibility in the process, their sense of ownership is maintained.

Similarly, it proved unrealistic and unworkable to expect every police officer to undertake assessments as part of their normal duties. Therefore arrangements were made for each officer to refer any child about whom they are concerned to an internal dedicated team, consisting of those officers covering missing persons, juvenile liaison, and domestic violence. These officers now undertake the common assessment with other health and education staff where appropriate.

Conclusion: Benefits of a common approach

The development of a common approach to the identification and assessment of children's needs has meant significant changes for children, families, and practitioners within North Lincolnshire. Children and families are now receiving a consistent assessment of and response to their needs, irrespective of which service they approach for help, and are no longer required to repeat their story at every stage. The assessment takes place when a concern is first raised rather than when the child reaches a crisis point. As each agency assesses need consistently, and as professionals trust each other's assessment of need, services are provided more promptly and coherently. Child welfare no longer receives high levels of inappropriate referrals "dressed up" as child protection cases requiring intensive investigation in order to access a service. There has been a 64% drop in child concern referrals following the introduction of the common assessment, as other agencies have taken responsibility for addressing the child's needs themselves. The subsequent reduction in children requiring child protection services can be seen in Figure 5. These figures are lower than the national average for England (United Kingdom Department of Health, 2003b).

Figure 5. Children on the Child Protection Register (per 1,000 population)

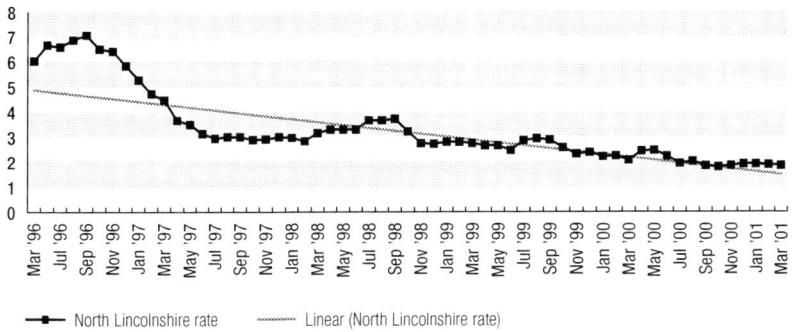

Most importantly, the reduction in unnecessary referrals has meant that some of the pressure on social services has been reduced and social workers have been able to move away from a single focus on the assessment of risk and devote more attention to providing services to children and families in need.

References

Adams, P. & Krauth, K. (1995). Working with families and communities: The patch approach. In P. Adams & K. Nelson (Eds.), *Reinventing human services* (pp. 87–108). Hawthorne, NY: Aldine de Gruyter.

Aldgate, J. & Bradley, M. (1999). *Supporting families through short-term fostering.* London: Her Majesty's Stationery Office.

Anderson, M. & Gobeil, S. (2003). *Recruitment and retention in child welfare services: A survey of Child Welfare League of Canada member agencies.* Ottawa, ON: Child Welfare League of Canada.

Andersson, G. (2002). *Child and family support in Sweden.* Paper presented at the Positive Possibilities for Child and Family Welfare conference, Partnerships for Children and Families Project, Faculty of Social Work, Wilfrid Laurier University, Waterloo, ON.

Bagley, C. & Young, L. (1999). Long-term evaluation of group counselling for women with a history of child sexual abuse: Focus on depression, self-esteem, suicidal behaviours and social support. In C. Bagley & K. Mallick (Eds.), *Child sexual abuse and adult offenders: new theory and research.* Aldershot, UK: Ashgate.

Baird, C. & Wagner, D. (2000). The relative validity of actuarial- and consensus-based risk assessment systems. *Children and Youth Services Review, 22,* 839–871.

Ball, J. & Pence, A.R. (1999). Beyond developmentally appropriate practice: Developing community and culturally appropriate practice. *Young Children, March,* 46–50.

Barber, J.G. & Dunstone, R. (in press). Evidence based social work in Australia. In B. Thyer and M. Kazi (Eds.), *International perspectives in evidence based practice.* New York: Sage.

Basch, C.E., Sliepcevich, E.M., Gold, R.S., Duncan, D.F., & Kolbe, L.J. (1985). Avoiding type III errors in health education programs evaluations. *Health Education Quarterly, 12*(4), 315–331.

British Columbia Ministry for Children and Families (1999). *Ministry for Children and Families' interest paper: Nuu-chah-nulth services to members off treaty settlement lands.* Victoria, BC: Author.

British Columbia Ministry for Children and Families (1997). *Report of the task force on safeguards for children and youth in foster or group home care.* Victoria, BC: Author.

British Columbia Ministry of Children and Family Development (2002). *April 2002 month-end CF&CS statistics: Aboriginal children in care, SWIS-MIS statistical extract files* Victoria, BC: Child Protection Division, Author.

Belsky, J. (1993). Etiology of child maltreatment: A developmental-ecological analysis. *Psychological Bulletin, 114,* 413–434.

Bering Pruzan, V. L. (1997). Denmark: Voluntary placements as a family support. In N. Gilbert (Ed.), *Combating child abuse: International perspectives and trends* (pp. 125–142). New York: Oxford University Press.

Bethea, L. (1999, March 15). Primary prevention of child abuse. *American Family Physician.* Retrieved from http://www.aafp.org/afp/990315ap/1577.html

Biglan, A. & Taylor, T. K. (2000). Why have we been more successful at reducing tobacco use than violent crime? *American Journal of Community Psychology, 28* (3), 269–302.

Bouchard. C (1999). The community as a participative learning environment: The case of Centraide of Greater Montreal 1,2,3, GO! Project. In D.P. Keating & Hertzman, C. (Eds.). *Developmental health and the wealth of nations,* (pp. 311–321). New York: The Guilford Press.

Brodsky, A. E. (1996). Resilient single mothers in risky neighborhoods: Negative psychological sense of community. *Journal of Community Psychology, 24*(4), 347–363.

Brun, C. & Rapp, R.C. (2001). Strengths-based case management: Individuals' perspectives on strengths and the case manager relationship. *Social Work, 46*(3), 278–288.

Brunson, L., Bouchard, C., & Larrivée, M.-C. (2003, June). *Applying the Communities That Care Model to a new context and focal issue: The experience of Boscoville 2000 and Projet Béluga in Montreal, Canada.* Presented at the biennial meeting of the Society for Community Research and Action, Las Vegas, New Mexico.

Camasso, M.J. & Jagannathan, R. (2000). Modeling the reliability and predictive validity of risk assessment in child welfare. *Children and Youth Services Review, 22,* 873–896.

Cameron, G. & Cadell, S. (1999). Empowering participation in prevention programs for disadvantaged children and families. *Canadian Journal of Community Mental Health. 18*(1), 105–122.

Cameron, G., Freymond, N., Cornfield, D., & Palmer, S. (2001). *Positive possibilities for child and family welfare: Options for expanding the Ango-American child protection paradigm.* Waterloo, ON: Partnerships for Child and Families Project, Faculty of Social Work, Wilfrid Laurier University.

Cameron, G., Hayward, K., Mckenzie, A., Hancock, K., & Jeffery, H. (1999). *Partnerships and programs: Service provider involvement in Better Beginnings, Better Futures.* Kingston, ON: Better Beginnings Research Coordination Unit, Queen's University.

Cameron, G., Karabanow, J., Peirson, L., Laurendeau, M.C., & Chamberland, C. (2001). Program implementation and replication. In I. Prilleltensky, G. Nelson, & L. Peirson (Eds.). *Promoting family wellness and preventing child maltreatment: Fundamentals for thinking and action,* (pp. 318–346). Toronto, ON: University of Toronto Press.

Canadian Council on Social Development (2002). *The progress of Canada's children.* Ottawa: Author.

Center on Urban Poverty and Social Change (n.d.) *Putting Cleveland on the map: A 10-year retrospective.* Cleveland, OH: Mandel School of Applied Social Sciences, Case Western University. Retrieved from http://povertycenter.cwru.edu/cupscretrospect.pdf

Children Act 1989. Elizabeth II. Chapter 41. London: Queen's Printer of Acts of Parliament.

Children and Young People's Unit (2001). *Building a strategy for children and young people.* Consultation document. London: Author.

Cliche, G. (1998). *Agissons en complice.* Quebec: Ministère de la Santé et des Services sociaux.

Constitution Act, 1867 (Originally *The British North America Act, 1867*) (UK 30 & 31 Victoria, C.3). Retrieved August 8, 2003 from http://www.solon.org/Constitutions/Canada/English/ca_1867.html

Cornell, S. & J.P. Kalt (1992). *Reloading the dice: Improving the chances for economic development on American Indian reservations.* Available online at http://www.ksg.harvard.edu/hpaied/res_main.htm

Coulthard, C., Duncan, K., Goranson, S., Hewson, L., Howe, P., Lee, K., et al. (2001). *Report on staff retention.* Toronto, ON: Children's Aid Society of Toronto.

Coulton, C., Korbin, J., Su, M., & Chow, J. (1995). Community level factors in child maltreatment rates. *Child Development, 66,* 1262–1276.

Courtney, M. E. (1998). The costs of child protection in the context of welfare reform. *Future of Children, 8*(1), 88–103.

Dagenais, C., Bastien, M.-F., Bégin, J., Bouchard, C., & Fortin, D. (2000). *Evaluation d'implantation et d'impact du projet d'intervention massive à l'enfance.* Montreal, QC: Les cahiers GRAVE.

Dahlberg, G., Moss, P., & Pence, A. (1999). *Beyond quality in early childhood education and care: Postmodern perspectives.* London: Falmer.

Daro, D. & Donnelly, A. C. (2002). Charting the waves of prevention: Two steps forward, one step back. *Child Abuse & Neglect, 26,* 731–742.

Doueck, H.J., Bronson, D.E., & Levine, M. (1992). Evaluating risk assessment implementation in child protection: Issues for consideration. *Child Abuse & Neglect, 16,* 637–646.

Doueck, H.J., Levine, M., & Bronson, D.E. (1990). *Final report of the Child at Risk Field System: Findings from Ontario County.* Buffalo, NY: State University of New York, Research Center for Children and Youth.

Drake, B. & Pandey, S. (1996) Understanding the relationship between neighborhood. *Child Abuse & Neglect, 20*(11), pp. 1003–1018.

Durlak, J.A. (1998). Why program implementation is important. *Journal of Prevention and Intervention in the Community, 17*(2), 5–18.

Durst, D. (1996). *First Nations self government: An annotated bibliography.* University of Regina: Faculty of Social Work Social Administration Research Unit.

English, D. J. (1998). The extent and consequences of child maltreatment. *Future of Children, 8*(1), 39–53.

Etherington. F. (2000a, October 23). Help when there is little hope. *The Record*, p. A6.

Etherington, F. (2000b, October 21). Setting limits on abuse. *The Record*, p. H1.

Éthier, L.S., Couture, G., & Lacharité, C. (in press). Risk factors associated with the chronicity of high potential for child abuse and neglect. *Family Violence*.

Éthier, L.S., Lemelin, J.P., & Désaulniers, R. (2003). *Rapport préliminaire inédit sur l'étude d'évaluation des familles négligentes en protection de la jeunesse (1992–2002)*. Université du Québec à Trois-Rivières: Groupe de recherche et d'intervention en négligence.

Farrow, F. (1997). *Building community partnerships for child protection: Getting from here to there.* Cambridge, MA: Harvard University, Malcolm Wiener Center for Social Policy. Retrieved from http://www.ksg.harvard.edu/socpol/farrow_3.4_final.pdf

Garbarino, J. & Kostelny, K. (1992). Child maltreatment as a community problem. *Child Abuse & Neglect, 16,* 455–464.

Garbarino, J. & Sherman, D. (1980). High-risk neighborhoods and high-risk families: The human ecology of child maltreatment. *Child Development, 51,* 188–198.

Garbarino, J. (1995). *Raising children in a socially toxic environment.* San Francisco: Jossey Bass.

Godenzi, A. & DePuy, J. (2001). Overcoming boundaries: A cross cultural inventory of primary prevention programs against wife abuse and child abuse. *The Journal of Primary Prevention, 21,* 455–475.

Government of Quebec (1998). Groupe de travail sur la révision du Manuel de référence sur la Loi sur la protection de la jeunesse. *Manuel de référence sur la protection de la jeunesse.* Quebec, QC: Ministère de la Santé et des Services sociaux.

Harden, B. J. (1998). Building bridges for children: Addressing the consequences of exposure to drugs and to the child welfare system. In R. L. Hampton, V. Senatore, & T. P. Gullotta (Eds.), *Substance abuse, family violence and child welfare: Bridging perspectives* (pp. 18–61), Vol. 10. Thousand Oaks, CA: Sage Publications.

Hardiker, P., Atkins, B., Barker, M., Brunton-Reed, S., Exton, K., Perry, M., et al. (2002). A framework for conceptualising need and its application to planning and providing services. In H. Ward & W. Rose (Eds.), *Approaches to needs assessment in children's services* (pp. 49–69). London: Jessica Kingsley Publishers.

Hardiker, P., Exton, K., & Barker, M. (1991) The social policy contexts of prevention in childcare. *British Journal of Social Work, 21*(4), 341–359.

Hélie, S., Renaud, J., Bouchard, C., Tourigny, M., Mayer, M., Lavergne, C., et al. (2002, July). *Risk of recurrence during the three year period following a report to Child Protective Services: Survival analysis of an urban cohort.* Poster session presented at the 14th International Congress of the International Society for Prevention of Child Abuse and Neglect, Denver, CO.

Hertzman, C., McLean, S.D., Kohen, D., Dunn, J., & Evans, T. (2002). *Early development in Vancouver: Report of the Community Asset Mapping Project (CAMP)*. Vancouver: University of British Columbia Early Human Learning Project. Retrieved from http://www.earlylearning.ubc.ca/vancouverreport.pdf

Hetherington, R., Cooper, A., Smith, P., & Wilford, G. (1997). *Protecting children: Messages from Europe*. Dorset, UK: Russell House Publishing Limited.

Hetherington, T. (1999). Child protection: A new approach in South Australia. *Child Abuse Review, 8*, 120–132.

Himmelman, A. T. (2001). On coalitions and the transformation of power relations: Collaborative betterment and collaborative empowerment. *American Journal of Community Psychology, 29*, 277–284.

Hogan, C.D. (1999). *Vermont communities count: Using results to strengthen services for families and children*. Baltimore: The Annie E. Casey Foundation.

Hyman, J. (2002). *Not quite chaos: Toward a more disciplined approach to community building*. Baltimore, MD: Annie E. Casey Foundation. Retrieved from http://www.aecf.org/tarc/spotlight/not_quite_chaos.pdf

Iglehart, A. (1994). Kinship foster care: Placement, service and outcome issues. *Social Service Review, 16*, 107–122.

Jones, L. M., Finkelhor, D. & Kopiec, K. (2001). Why is sexual abuse declining? A survey of state child protection administrators. *Child Abuse & Neglect, 25,* 1139–1158.

Kamerman, S.B. & Kahn A.J. (1990). Is CPS driving child welfare: Where do go from here? *Public Welfare, 48,* 9–12.

Karen, R. (1990). Becoming attached. *The Atlantic Monthly* (February), pp. 35–70.

Kempe, C. H., Silverman, F., Steele, B. Droegemuller, W, Silver, H. (1962). The battered child syndrome. *Journal of the American Medical Association, 181*: 17–24.

King, M. (1995). Law's healing of children's hearings: The paradox moves north. *Journal of Social Policy, 24*(3), 315–340.

Kline, D. & Overstreet, H. (1972). *Foster care of children.* New York: Child Welfare League of America.

Kordesh, R. (1995). *Irony and hope in the emerging family policies: A case for family empowerment associations.* Waltham, MA: Brandeis University Civic Practices Network. Retrieved from http://www.cpn.org/topics/families/irony.html

Kretzmann, J. P. & McKnight, J. L. (1993). *Building communities from the inside out: A path toward finding and mobilizing a community's assets.* Chicago, IL: ACTA.

Kuhn, T. (1968). *The structure of scientific revolutions.* Chicago: University of Chicago Press.

Larivière, C., Bernier, D., & Lapierre, J. (2000). *Les transformations des Centres jeunesse de Montréal et de Québec.* Rapport de recherche. Montreal, QC: Institut de recherche pour le développement social des jeunes.

Lessard, C. (2002). *Indicateurs repères à l'application de la loi de la protection de la jeunesse.* Montreal: Les Centres jeunesse de Montréal.

Luckock, B., Vogler, R., & Keating, H. (1997). The Belgian Flemish child protection system—Confidentiality, voluntarism and coercion. *Child and Family Law Quarterly, 9*(2), 101–113.

MacDonald, K. (2000). *First Nations Summit action committee for First Nations children and families: Discussion paper, phase two, options to address issues identified in phase one.* North Vancouver, BC: First Nations Summit.

Macleod, J. (2000). Programs for the promotion of family wellness and the prevention of child maltreatment: A meta-analytic review. *Child Abuse & Neglect, 24*(9), 1127–1149.

Maluccio, A.N. (1990). Family preservation services and the social work practice sequence. In J.K. Whittaker, J. Kinney, E.M. Tracy, & C. Booth (Eds.), *Reaching high-risk families: Intensive family preservation in human services. Modern applications of social work* (pp. 113–126). Hawthorne, NY: Aldine de Gruyter.

Maresca, J. (1995). Mediating child protection cases. *Child Welfare. LXXIV*(3), 731–742.

Martinez, L. (1987). Illinois presents its child protection risk assessment instrument. In T. Tatara (Ed.), *A summary of the highlights of the National Roundtable on CPS Risk Assessment and Family Systems Assessment* (pp. 13–48), Washington, DC: American Public Welfare Association.

McDonald, R.J. & P. Ladd (2000, June). *First Nations child and family services joint national policy review: Final report.* Prepared for the Assembly of First Nations with First Nations child and family service agency representatives in partnership with the Department of Indian Affairs and Northern Development. Ottawa, ON: Assembly of First Nations.

McKnight, J. L. (1987). Regenerating community. *Social Policy, 17* (3), 5458. Available from http://www.cpn.org/cpn/sections/topics/community/civic_perspectives/regen_comm.html

McNeilly, G. K. (1997). Mediation and child protection: An Ontario perspective. *Family and Conciliation Courts Review, 35*(2), 206–222.

Nunnally, E. (1967). *Psychometric Theory.* New York: McGraw Hill.

O'Brien, V. (2001). Relative care: A different type of foster care—implications for practice. In G. Kelly & R. Gilligan (Eds.), *Issues in foster care: Policy, practice and research.* London: Jessica Kingsley Publishers.

Ontario Association of Children's Aid Societies (2002). *Funding and Services Analysis, April 1, 2001 to March 31 2002.* Toronto: Author.

Ontario's children's aid societies face severe cash crunch, debt. (2003, January 28). *The Record.*

Pancer, S.M. & Cameron, G. (1994). Resident participation in the Better Beginnings, Better Futures prevention project: The impacts of involvement. *Canadian Journal of Community Mental Health. 13*, 197–211.

Parker, R., Ward, H., Jackson, S., Aldgate, J., & Wedge, P. (1991). *Looking After Children: Assessing outcomes in child care.* London: Her Majesty's Stationery Office.

Peel, M. & Ward, H. (1997). *The Refocusing Children's Services Initiative: A literature review.* Unpublished report. Leicester, UK: Leicester University.

Peirson, L., Laurendeau, M.-C., & Chamberland, C. (2001). Context, contributing factors, and consequences. In I. Prilleltensky, G. Nelson, & L. Peirson (Eds.), *Promoting family wellness and preventing child maltreatment: Fundamentals for thinking and action* (pp. 41–123). Toronto: University of Toronto Press.

Pelton, L.H. (1990). Resolving the cases in child welfare. *Public Welfare, 48,* 19–25.

Pires, S. A. (1993). *International child welfare systems: Report of a workshop.* Washington, DC: National Academy Press.

Potvin, J.M. & Dionne, M. (2003). L'intervention en protection: L'art de la relation d'aide en contexte d'autorité. *Défi jeunesse, 9*(3), 25–29.

Prilleltensky, I., Peirson, L., & Nelson, G. (2001). Mapping the terrain: Framework for promoting family wellness and preventing child maltreatment. I. Prilleltensky, G. Nelson, & L. Peirson (Eds.), *Promoting family wellness and preventing child maltreatment: Fundamentals for thinking and action* (pp. 3–40). Toronto: University of Toronto Press.

Groupe de travail sur la révision du Manuel de référence sur la Loi sur la protection de la jeunesse (1998). *Manuel de référence sur la protection de la jeunesse.* Québec: Ministère de la santé et des services sociaux.

Ratiner, C. (2000). Child abuse treatment research. In R. M. Reece (Ed.), *Treatment of child abuse: Common ground for mental health, medical and legal practitioners* (pp. 362–370). Baltimore: The John Hopkins University Press.

Regehr, C., Leslie, B., Howe, P., & Chau, S. (2000). *Stressors in child welfare practice*, Toronto, ON: Centre for Applied Research, University of Toronto and Children's Aid Society of Toronto. Available from http://www.cecw-cepb.ca/DocsEng/Stressors.pdf

Roosa, M. W., Jones, S., Tein, J.-Y., & Cree, W. (2003). Prevention science and neighborhood influences on low-income children's development: Theoretical and methodological issues. *American Journal of Community Psychology, 31* (1/2), 55–72.

Rossi, P., Schuerman, J., & Budde, S. (1996). *Understanding child maltreatment decisions and those who make them.* Chapin Hall Center for Children, University of Chicago.

Royal Commission on Aboriginal Peoples (1996). *Report of the Royal Commission on*

Aboriginal Peoples. Available online at http://www.ainc-inac.gc.ca/ch/rcap/sg/sg1_e.html#0

Rutman, D., Barlow, A., Alusik, D., Hubberstey, C., & Brown, E. (2003). Supporting young people's transitions from government care. In K. Kufeldt & B. MacKenzie (Eds.) *Child welfare: Connecting research, policy and practice,* (pp. 227–238). Waterloo, ON: Wilfrid Laurier University Press

Salzer, M.S. & Bickman, L. (1997). Delivering effective children's services in the community: Reconsidering the benefits of system interventions. *Applied and Preventive Psychology, 6*(1), 1–13.

Sampson, R.J. (2001). How do communities undergird or undermine human development? Relevant contexts and social mechanisms. In A. Booth & A.C. Crouter (Eds.), *Does it take a village? Community effects on children, adolescents and families.* Mahwah, NJ: Lawrence Erlbaum Associates.

Sampson, R.J., Raudenbush, S., & Earls, F. (1997). Neighborhoods and violent crime: A multilevel study of collective efficacy. *Science, 277,* 918–924.

Sandau-Beckler, P., Salcido, R., Beckler, M.-J.; Mannes, M., & Beck, M. (2002). Infusing family-centered values into child protective practice. *Children and Youth Services Review, 24*(9/10), 719–741.

Schene, P. (2002). *Forming and sustaining partnerships.* Paper presented at the Positive Possibilities for Child and Family Welfare conference, Partnerships for Children and Families Project, Faculty of Social Work, Wilfrid Laurier University, Waterloo, ON.

Schmidt, D.E. (2001, March). *The Child, Family and Community Services Act British Columbia: Judicial case conferences.* Materials prepared for the National Judicial Insititute, Vancouver, BC.

Schorr, L.B. (1997). *Common Purpose. Strengthening families and neighborhoods to rebuild America.* New York: Anchor Books.

Schorr, L.B., Sylvester, K., & Dunkle, M. (1999). *Strategies to achieve a common purpose: Tools for turning good ideas into good policies.* Washington, DC: The Policy Exchange, Institute for Educational Leadership. Retrieved from http://www.iel.org/pubs/pubs/strategies.pdf

Secretariat to the Federal/Provincial/Territorial Working Group on Child and Family Services Information (2002). *Child Welfare in Canada—2000.* Ottawa: National Clearinghouse on Family Violence.

South Australia Department of Human Services (2002). *Practice audit. Progress report.* Adelaide, Australia: Author.

Stack, Carol. (1997). *All our kin: Strategies for survival in a black community.* New York: Basic Books.

Statham, J. & Aldgate, J. (2003). From legislation to practice: Learning from the Children Act 1989 research program. *Children and Society, 17,* 149–156.

Swift, K. J. (1995). *Manufacturing 'bad mothers': A critical perspective on child neglect.* Toronto, ON: University of Toronto Press.

Thorpe, D. (1997). *Report on Child Protection Referrals to North Lincolnshire Council Social Services Directorate.* Unpublished report. Lancaster: Lancaster University.

Tourigny, M., Jacob, M., Poirier, M.-A., Julien, A. & Doray, A. (in press). Les décisions prises en contexte de protection de la jeunesse au Québec : facteurs associés et différences régionales. Montreal: Centre de liaison sur l'intervention et la prévention psychosociales.

Tourigny, M., Mayer, M., Wright, J., Lavergne, C., Hélie, S., Trocmé, N., et al. (2002). *Étude sur l'incidence et les caractéristiques des situations d'abus, de négligence, d'abandon et de troubles de comportement sérieux signalées à la direction de la protection de la jeunesse au Québec (ÉIQ).* Montreal: Centre de liaison sur l'intervention et la prévention psychosociale.

Trocmé, N. & Wolfe, D. (2001). *Child maltreatment in Canada: Canadian incidence study of reported child abuse and neglect (Selected results).* Ottawa, ON: Minister of Public Works and Government Services Canada.

Trocmé, N., Fallon, B., MacLaurin, B., Copp, B. (2002). *The changing face of child welfare investigations in Ontario: Ontario incidence studies of reported child abuse and neglect (OIS 1993/1998)*. Toronto, ON: Centre of Excellence in Child Welfare, Faculty of Social Work, University of Toronto. Available from http://cecw-cepb.ca

Trocmé, N., Fallon, B., MacLaurin, B., Daciuk, J., Bartholomew, S., Ortiz, J., et al. (2002). *1998 Ontario Incidence Study of Reported Child Abuse and Neglect (OIS 1998)*. Toronto, ON: Centre of Excellence for Child Welfare, Faculty of Social Work, University of Toronto.

Trocmé, N., Knott, T., & Roy, C. (2003). *An overview of differential response models*. Information sheet. Toronto, ON: Centre of Excellence for Child Welfare, Faculty of Social Work, University of Toronto.

Trocmé, N., MacLaurin, B., Fallon, B., Daciuk, J., Billingsley, D., Tourigny, et al. (2001). *Canadian incidence study of reported child abuse and neglect: Final report*. Ottawa, ON: Minister of Public Works and Government Services Canada.

Trocmé, N., McPhee, D., Kwan Tam, K., & Hay, T. (1994). *1993 Ontario Incidence Study of Reported Child Abuse and Neglect*. Toronto: Institute for the Prevention of Child Abuse/Bell Canada Child Welfare Research Unit, Faculty of Social Work, University of Toronto.

Trocmé, N., Nutter, B., MacLaurin, B., & Fallon, B. (1999). *Child welfare outcome indicator matrix*. Toronto, ON: Bell Canada Child Welfare Research Unit, University of Toronto.

Tunnard, T. (2002). Matching needs and services: Emerging themes from its application in different social care settings. In H. Ward & W. Rose (Eds.), *Approaches to needs assessment in children's services* (pp. 99–126). London: Jessica Kingsley Publishers.

Tuomisto, R. & Vuori-Karvia, E. (1997). Child protection in Finland. In M. Harder & K. Pringle (Eds.), *Protecting children in Europe: Towards a new millennium* (pp. 77–100). Aalborg, Denmark: Aalborg University Press.

Union of BC Indian Chiefs (2002). *Calling forth our future: Options for the exercise of indigenous peoples' authority in child welfare*. Available online from http://www.ubcic.bc.ca/docs/UBCIC_OurFuture.pdf

United Kingdom Department of Health (1995). *Child protection, Messages from research*. London: Her Majesty's Stationery Office.

United Kingdom Department of Health (2003a). *The integrated children's system.* Available from http://www.doh.gov.uk/integratedchildrenssystem/htm

United Kingdom Department of Health (2003b). *Referrals, assessments and children and young people on Child Protection Register.* Available from http://www.doh.gov.uk/public/stats3.htm

United Kingdom Department of Health, Department for Education and Employment, Home Office (2000). *Framework for the Assessment of Children in Need and their Families.* London: Her Majesty's Stationery Office.

Waldfogel, J. (2001a). Differential response: A new paradigm for child protective services. In J. Waldfogel (Ed.), *The future of child protection: How to break the cycle of abuse and neglect* (137–160). Cambridge, MA: Harvard University Press.

Waldfogel, J. (Ed.) (2001b). *The future of child protection: How to break the cycle of abuse and neglect.* Cambridge, MA: Harvard University Press.

Ward, H. & Peel M. (2002). An inter-agency approach to needs assessment. In H. Ward & W. Rose (Eds.), *Approaches to needs assessment in children's services* (pp. 217–234). London: Jessica Kingsley Publishers.

Ward, H. & Rose, W. (Eds.) (2002). *Approaches to needs assessment in children's services.* London: Jessica Kingsley Publishers.

Ward, H. (Ed.) (1995). *Looking After Children: Research into practice.* London: Her Majesty's Stationery Office.

Weber, M. W. (1998). Commentary 4: How we can better protect children from abuse and neglect. *The Future of Children, 8* (1), 129–132.

White, D., Jobin L., McCann, D., & Morin, P. (2002). *L'action intersectorielle en santé mentale.* Ste-Foy, QC: Publications du Québec.

Wilford, G., Hetherington, R., & Piquardt, R. (1997). *Families ask for help: Parental perceptions of child welfare and child protection services—An Anglo-German study.* London: Brunel University.

Wolff, R. (1997). Germany: A nonpunitive model. In N. Gilbert (Ed.), *Combatting child abuse: International perspectives and trends* (pp. 212–231). New York: Oxford University Press.

Woodward, L. J. & Fergusson, D. M. (2002). Parent, child, and contextual predictors of childhood physical punishment. *Infant and Child Development, 11,* 213–235.

Contributors

Suzanne Anselmo is currently Senior Manager of Intergovernmental Initiatives for Alberta Children's Services. Educated at Georgetown University in international law and human rights theory and at the University of Virginia in political philosophy and international relations, Suzanne Anselmo has been able to apply this knowledge in the area of social policy development. Over the last 15 years, she has worked in the areas of early childhood development, services to persons with disabilities, community capacity building, and supports for persons requiring income assistance. Most recently, Suzanne has been part of the project team supporting the development and implementation of the Alberta Response Model, whose goal is to transform outcomes for children, youth, and families receiving child welfare services.

Jim Barber is currently Dean of Social Work at the University of Toronto. He holds post-graduate qualifications in social work and psychology and has extensive experience as a practitioner, including in street work with young homeless people and alcoholic men. He has also lived and worked with Australian Aborigines in the Australian desert, with patients in a hospice for the dying, with high school students in an inner city high school, and with schizophrenia sufferers in a psychiatric hospital. Jim Barber began his academic career at James Cook University in tropical North Queensland and has since worked at a number of Australian universities, including, La Trobe University in Melbourne where he became the only social worker in La Trobe's history to be promoted to the rank of Reader. Jim lists among his various research projects over the years: the development of social modeling programs for Australian Aboriginal children, the development of a relapse prevention program within the Australian prison system, and a large tracking study of children in foster care. He is very committed to evidence-based practice and to outcome evaluation generally.

Cindy Blackstock, BA (University of British Columbia), MM (McGill University) is a member of the Gitksan Nation and has worked in the field of child and family services for over 20 years. In her current capacity, Cindy is honoured to be the Executive Director of the First Nations Child and Family

Caring Society of Canada (FNCFCS). This national organization seeks to promote and support the works and knowledge of First Nations child and family service agencies and regional organizations in Canada by providing research, professional development, and networking services. Cindy was privileged to participate in numerous provincial and national research projects and task forces. These include appointments to the Assembly of First Nations/Department of Indian Affairs and Northern Development National Policy Review Committee, the Centre of Excellence for Child Welfare Steering Committee, and the First Nations Summit Child Welfare Committee.

Maurice D. Brubacher is the Executive Director of Family and Children's Services of Guelph and Wellington County and has over 25 years of extensive experience in all areas of child welfare services. With a Master of Social Work, his training and experience includes clinical service, community development, social administration, and Native services. Moe has a passionate commitment to the development of programs and services that keep children safe while supporting families to protect and care for their own children wherever possible. He believes that child welfare is a collective community responsibility and has done a lot to mobilize formal and informal community resources to support high-risk families. Moe has also has provided leadership and support to Tikinagan Child and Family Services, a Native children's aid society in northwestern Ontario for the past four years, assisting with a major redevelopment process and the establishment of a customary care service model.

Liesette Brunson, PhD, is Project Coordinator of Boscoville 2000. She obtained her doctorate in community psychology and developmental psychology from the University of Illinois at Urbana-Champaign in 1999. Her research interests focus on community social capital, the social integration of adolescents and young families, and the development of innovative interventions to promote the optimal development of children, youth, and families. Since completing her PhD, she has focused on developing community-based research projects that examine the quality of environments for families and the development and evaluation of local social innovations. She has communicated these research results to community members and decision-makers as well as to the scientific community, writing numerous research reports for community audiences as well as publishing in internationally recognized scientific journals. Dr. Brunson is currently Project Coordinator for Projet Béluga, a program that that seeks to prevent child abuse and neglect using a strategy of local community mobilisation.

Luc Cadieux received a master's degree in criminology from the University of Ottawa in 1978 and a master's in project management from the *Université du Québec en Outaouais* in 1994. Mr. Cadieux has worked for Outaouais youth centres (*Centres jeunesse*) in western Quebec since 1978, where he has held a number of positions, including youth liaison, youth protection worker, chief of non-institutional services (foster families), assistant director of child protection, and director of regional services. He has been a Director of Youth Protection since September 1997. He is a firm believer in community participation and the inclusion of vulnerable children and families in the provision of services for the population as a whole and that collaboration and partnership are solid values in the development of quality services for children and youth in difficulty.

Gary Cameron is a professor with the Faculty of Social Work, Wilfrid Laurier University (WLU) in Waterloo, Ontario. He has been the principal investigator for a variety of major research and demonstration projects focusing on interventions with vulnerable children and families, including, studies of family support in child welfare, parent mutual aid organizations, intensive family preservation services, promising programs and organizational realities in child welfare, and project/program development in the Better Beginnings, Better Futures Prevention Project. He served as Director of the Centre for Social Welfare Studies at WLU from 1986 until 1996. Currently, he is the Project Director for the Partnerships for Children and Families Project, a community-university research alliance. Dr. Cameron has authored numerous research reports, is the co-editor of four volumes and has co-authored two books as well as numerous book chapters and journal articles. His latest publications focus on program models for disadvantaged adolescents, program implementation and replication challenges, international comparisons of systems of child and family welfare, and the experiences of disadvantaged families involved with child protection and residential care services.

Claire Chamberland has a PhD in psychology from the Université du Québec à Montréal. Claire is a full professor at the School of Social Work, Université de Montréal. She was the director of the Institut de recherche pour le développement social des jeunes in Montreal from 1995 to 2001. She is Co-director of the Centre of Excellence for Child Welfare as well as Co-director of the Groupe de recherche et d'action sur la victimisation des enfants. Claire has contributed to the development, implementation, and evaluation of innovative prevention and promotion programs for children and families. Her research interests include family violence, intersectoral and multidisciplinary approaches, and the continuum of social action and innovation in child and family issues.

Ellen Chant has a background in nursing and after working as a Registered General Nurse in an accident and emergency department, she went on to qualify as a Health Visitor in 1993 and subsequently a Community Practice Teacher in 1996. It was her work with vulnerable children and families that motivated her interest in the research and piloting of an inter-agency assessment process within North Lincolnshire, undertaken by Harriet Ward and Mark Peel. After a successful piloting of the assessment, Ellen took up the post of Common Assessment Development Co-ordinator in 1999 to extend the use of the Common Assessment throughout North Lincolnshire. Her role includes the strategic and operational development of the assessment of children in need as well as being a trainer and facilitator for professionals in the Common Assessment process. North Lincolnshire's Common Assessment for children in need has been highlighted as an innovative and successful achievement in the development of integration within children's services.

Gilles Clavel has a master's degree in criminology from the University of Ottawa and a master's in public administration from the *École Nationale d'Administration Publique*. He began his career with a community organization for ex-offenders. From 1978 to 1984, he taught at both the university and college levels. In 1979, he started as a front-line worker at the same time as the introduction of Quebec's new youth protection law and finished as a Director of Youth Protection. For six years, he was the executive director of the *Centres jeunesse de l'Outaouais*. For a number of years, he has been engaged in the development of services for children at risk and in working collaboratively with community partners.

Directors of Child Welfare are designated by the minister responsible for social services in each province and territory to oversee and administer each jurisdiction's child welfare legislation. The provincial and territorial Directors of Child Welfare meet regularly as a group to discuss issues of common concern and interest and to undertake joint projects in an effort to enhance child welfare service delivery and promote the prevention of child maltreatment.

Peter Dudding is Executive Director of the Child Welfare League of Canada and has held senior management positions in child welfare, public health, and international development during the past 30 years. He has a passionate interest in children's services and is dedicated to improving the quality of life for children and youth. He has a master's degree in social work and recently completed a Master of Management in national voluntary sector leadership. Mr. Dudding is Co-director of the Centre of Excellence for Child Welfare. He is currently involved with conducting applied research, establishing best practice models, policy and program development, evaluating outcomes, advocacy, disseminating information, building awareness, and social marketing. Mr. Dudding has worked with Aboriginal and multicultural populations in Canada and internationally.

Diana J. English completed a PhD in social welfare at the University of Washington in 1985. Since 1987 she has been Director of the Office of the Children's Administration Research (OCAR) with the Washington State Department of Social and Health Services, Children's Administration. During the past 15 years, OCAR has conducted over 30 research projects related to public child welfare issues including studies related to risk assessment, child protection system decision making, re-referral, recurrence, placement stability, and re-entry and the effectiveness of services. Dr. English has been researching the effectiveness of alternative response systems since 1989 and has published numerous articles and reports on this and other child welfare related topics. In addition, Dr. English has been a member of national committees addressing questions of interest related to public child welfare including, a National Research Council Committee examining the effectiveness of interventions in family violence including, domestic violence and child maltreatment.

John D. Fluke, PhD, has been the Director of Research for Walter R. McDonald & Associates, Inc. since 1999 and has over 20 years of experience is social service delivery research, especially in the area of child welfare. His responsibilities emphasize his background in the development and analysis of social services performance data, decision support technology, and evaluation design and implementation. Prior to joining Walter R. McDonald & Associates, Dr. Fluke was employed in a similar capacity by the American Humane Association where he directed numerous state and national projects. Throughout his entire career he has been involved in the collection and analysis of child maltreatment reporting data for the US federal government up through his current analytic role on the National Child Abuse and Neglect Data System. He has published widely in the field, presented at numerous national and international forums, and participated on several advisory, policy making, and corporate boards. Dr. Fluke holds BA and MA degrees in anthropology from the University of Northern Colorado and the Pennsylvania State University respectively. His PhD is in the area of organizational decision science from the Union Institute Graduate School.

Debra Foxcroft is a member of the Tseshaht Tribe and has been a central force in British Columbia First Nations child and family services. As a senior manager of Community Human Services for the Nuu-chah-nulth Tribal Council in the early 1980s, she was involved in activities which led to the delegated authority of child welfare and the creation of USMA Nuu-chah-nulth Child and Family Services. In 1992, Debra was project coordinator for an Indian child and family services standards project which resulted in much needed discussion and documentation of Indian child welfare standards of services. She is the Chair of the First Nations Child Welfare Committee of the First Nations Summit, Chair of the Vancouver Island Aboriginal Transition Team and Co-chair of Vancouver Island Planning for the BC Ministry for Children and Families. She is currently completing a bachelor of social work at the University of Victoria.

Nancy Freymond is a doctoral student at Wilfrid Laurier University and a research associate with the Partnerships for Children and Families Project, a community-university research alliance, dedicated to fostering appropriate helping relationships in child welfare. Her research centres on placement experiences from the perspective of both the child welfare worker and the birth parents. She is the co-author of a paper that examines positive possibilities for child and family welfare and sole author of papers on international comparison of practice in child protection, worker experiences in making placement decisions, and parents' experiences with child placement. Nancy's interest in this research stems from her experiences as a front-line child protection worker in Ontario.

Phil Goodman has dedicated his career to working with children, families, and communities, spearheading change as a child welfare specialist in a variety of roles, including senior official and political advisor. His pursuits in the field of social work span over 30 years. Phil has been with Alberta Children's Services since April 2000, first as director of the Best Practices Branch and currently as Assistant Deputy Minister of the Community Strategies Division. Prior to working in Alberta, Phil was employed in Manitoba as the director of child welfare and was a leader in the child welfare transformation. He has worked as executive director of Child and

Family Services with Manitoba Family Services; the Manitoba Adolescent Treatment Centre; and the Manitoba Foster Parents' Association.

Helen Jones has a background in social work with children and families which includes practice, the management of family placement services, and policy development and implementation. For the past nine years she has been a professional advisor on child welfare policy at the UK Department of Health and has worked on the development of outcome and performance measures for children's services, the Looking After Children system, and the Integrated Children's System.

Della Knoke is a PhD student at the Faculty of Social Work at the University of Toronto and a Research Assistant at the Centre of Excellence for Child Welfare. She attained a BSc with a specialty in psychology and an MA in applied (school) psychology. Her clinical experience includes treating anxiety, stress-related disorders, and alcohol dependence. In addition, she has several years experience in the assessment of psychological and cognitive functioning in children and adults who have been affected by medical conditions or physical trauma. Della has extensive research experience and has co-authored several peer-reviewed publications, primarily in addictions and psychopharmacology. Her research interests in child welfare include identifying factors associated with recurrent maltreatment, the development of empirically-based risk assessment approaches, and the evaluation of outcomes for children and families receiving child welfare services.

Jasma Narayan is currently a social work consultant and trainer and recently retired as executive director of Better Beginnings, Better Futures in Guelph, Ontario. After immigrating from Guyana with her family in 1965, Jassy chose to stay at home to take care of her three young girls and provide private child care to many other young children. Later she undertook the Early Childhood Education Diploma program at Conestoga College in Kitchener, Ontario and went on to earn a BA and a master's in social work in community development and social planning at Wilfrid Laurier University in Waterloo, Ontario. Jassy has volunteered for a number of community groups, including, the YWCA, the Social Planning Council, Anselma House, the Centre for Research and Education in Human Services, Calvin Church Refugee Resettlement Committee, Women in Crisis, Ontario Immigrant and Visible Minority's Network, and Focus for Ethnic Women. She has received many community service awards, including the Queen's 50th

Jubilee Medal, the Ontario Provincial Government Award, Women of Distinction (Kitchener-Waterloo and Guelph), Guelph Police Services Award, and the Rotary Club of Guelph Paul Harris Fellowship.

Russ Pickford is in his thirteenth year with the Government of Alberta, Ministry of Children's Services. As Project Manager for the Alberta Response Model, Russ is in the enviable position of being part of a dynamic service delivery change that seldom happens in one's career. Russ is a recent addition to the Accountability and Program Support Division in the department, having previously been the manager of the Spruce Grove Child and Family Service Centre. Having also worked as a screener, investigator, case manager, and supervisor, Russ brings the front-line perspective and application needs to the forefront of the Alberta Response Model.

Catherine Roy has a PhD in social work. Social support of vulnerable children and their families, development of protective factors and resiliency within these families, as well as children's views of maltreatment constitute her main research interests. Since completing her doctoral degree, Catherine Roy has been the scientific coordinator for the Centre of Excellence for Child Welfare.

Nico Trocmé is an Associate Professor at the Faculty of Social Work, University of Toronto and the Director of Centre of Excellence for Child Welfare and of the Bell Canada Child Welfare Research Unit. Dr. Trocmé is the principle investigator for Canadian Incidence Study of Reported Child Abuse and Neglect (CIS), the first national survey of investigated maltreatment ever conducted in Canada. Additional research activities include pilot testing a national framework for tracking child welfare outcome indicators funded by the provincial and territorial Directors of Child Welfare and Human Resources Development Canada, comparative analysis of maltreatment rates in Canada and the US, the development and evaluation of a home based comprehensive treatment model in situations of chronic neglect, and a survey of risk and resilience for youth receiving child welfare services. Dr. Trocmé was as a member of the Minister's Panel of Experts on Child Protection in Ontario, presented expert evidence at several coroner inquests, and has been assisting in the development of a province-wide client information system that will track outcomes for children and families receiving child welfare services. Prior to completing his PhD, Dr. Trocmé worked for five years as a child welfare and children's mental health social worker.

Harriet Ward is a Senior Research Fellow in Social Sciences at Loughborough University and Director of the Centre for Child and Family Research, which conducts policy-relevant research on services for vulnerable children and adults. There are currently four main areas of work within the centre, with individual studies funded by government departments, charities, and national and local child welfare agencies: (i) cohort studies of outcomes for children in need; (ii) development of methodologies for identifying need and assessing outcome; (iii) costing child welfare services; (iv) young carers and their parents. Much of Dr. Ward's research has developed from the Looking After Children project, which she has led since 1992. This program for gathering information, monitoring the services and assessing outcomes for children looked after away from home has now been implemented throughout the United Kingdom, in several Canadian provinces and Australian states, and in parts of Eastern Europe, with pilots underway in Sweden, New Zealand, and Germany.

Ying-Ying T. Yuan, PhD, is Senior Vice President of Walter R. McDonald & Associates, Inc. Dr. Yuan conducts research on human services program management and service delivery for federal, state, and local governments, private non-profit agencies, and foundations. She received her doctorate from the Department of Social Relations, Harvard University. Dr. Yuan is nationally recognized as an evaluator and child welfare expert. She has been the lead evaluator for several cluster evaluations including several latchkey children programs in California, several family preservation programs in Connecticut and California, perinatal services in eight communities, and adoption reform in nine states for the W.K. Kellogg Foundation. Currently, she leads an evaluation of educational systems reform for the W.K. Kellogg Foundation and recently completed the National Study of Child Protective Services Systems and Reform Efforts. She has been the Technical Director of the National Child Abuse and Neglect Data System (NCANDS) since 1990. In that role she directs a team of analysts and technical assistance providers who work directly with the 50 states and the District of Columbia.